The Great American
Grilling Book

★ ★ ★

The Great American Grilling Book

Contents

FISH AND SHELLFISH
★ 95 ★

BURGERS AND KABOBS
★ 111 ★

SIDE DISHES
★ 145 ★

DESSERTS
★ 165 ★

Time Inc. Home Entertainment

Publisher Richard Fraiman
General Manager Steven Sandonato
Executive Director, Marketing Services Carol Pittard
Director, Retail & Special Sales Tom Mifsud
Director, New Product Development Peter Harper
Assistant Director, Brand Marketing Laura Adam
Associate Counsel Helen Wan
Senior Brand Manager, TWRS/M Holly Oakes
Design & Prepress Manager Anne-Michelle Gallero
Book Production Manager Susan Chodakiewicz
Assistant Manager, Product Marketing Nina Fleishman

Special thanks Alexandra Bliss, Glenn Buonocore, Margaret Hess, Suzanne Janso, Robert Marasco, Dennis Marcel, Brooke Reger, Mary Sarro-Waite, Ilene Schreider, Adriana Tierno, Alex Voznesenskiy

ISBN 10: 1-60320-020-7
ISBN 13: 978-1-60320-020-2
LOC #: 2008900479

Text pages printed and bound in Mexico

We welcome your comments and suggestions.
Please write to us at: Omaha Steaks Great American Grilling
Attention: Book Editors
PO Box 11016
Des Moines, IA 50336-1016

If you would like to order any of our hardcover Collector's Edition books, please call us at 1-800-327-6388. (Monday through Friday, 7:00 a.m.— 8:00 p.m. or Saturday, 7:00 a.m.—6:00 p.m. Central Time).

Omaha Steaks International, Inc.

Senior Vice President and Chief Marketing Officer Todd Simon

Special thanks Omaha Steaks Test Kitchen; Omaha Creative Group: Advertising, Marketing and Public Relations

Downtown Bookworks Inc.

President Julie Merberg
Editor Sara Newberry
Recipes John Harrisson and Judith Choate
Design Patricia Fabricant

Photography Jerry Errico/jerryerrico.com
with the exception of page 16 © Omaha Steaks

Special thanks Patty Brown, Pam Abrams, Sarah Parvis, Kate Gibson

Grilling has come a long way in a very short time. A generation or two ago, options were pretty limited when it came to grilling recipes, techniques, and equipment. Now, as its popularity has soared, grilling has entered the mainstream. For many, home grilling has become a badge of honor, a genuine source of pride and enjoyment. Perhaps this can be attributed to our innate "grilling genes" kicking in as we rediscover what is probably the oldest cooking technique of all.

There are so many reasons why grilling has undergone a renaissance. It's the perfect way to cook at home while avoiding the heat and confines of the kitchen. We can enjoy the fresh air of the outdoors and revel in the aromas of grilling without worrying about setting off smoke alarms. Grilling is adaptable, versatile, and controllable (and who doesn't feel powerful when building a fire)?

The recipes in this book range from traditional favorites, including some classics from the Omaha Steaks archives, to new and innovative grilling combinations that reflect the far superior availability, diversity, and quality of ingredients compared to twenty or thirty years ago. There is truly something here for everyone and for every occasion—we have even included some dessert recipes, which you might not expect from a grilling book. So turn the page, and let's get grilling!

All about Cooking with Fire

Is there a difference between grilling and barbecuing? Most people use the terms interchangeably, but they are really two distinct cooking methods.

GRILLING VS. BARBECUING

Grilling is the most popular method of cooking over flame, and the term refers to cooking over a direct heat source, such as wood, charcoal, or gas. Grilling usually involves high heat (500°F or more) and short cooking times (20 minutes or less). The high heat creates a caramelized crust that seals in a food's natural juices. Grilling can be done with or without a cover; cooking times are shorter on a covered grill because the temperature is higher. A covered grill also enhances the smoky flavor, especially if you grill over wood or use wood chips. It is necessary to vent a covered grill to prevent the fire from going out.

Barbecuing involves lower, indirect heat (250°F or less) and longer cooking time. Larger, less tender cuts of meat such as beef ribs, roasts, brisket, and whole fish or poultry are all ideal for barbecuing, which breaks down the tough connective tissue in much the same way that roasting or braising does. Barbecuing is the preferred method when the object is to infuse foods with the complex tones and flavors of smoke.

When barbecuing, place food over a drip pan to prevent flare-ups. For best results, place a flame-proof container of water inside the grill to add humidity and prevent food from drying out.

OTHER GRILL-COOKING METHODS

There are a number of variations on the basic technique of cooking over flame and fire.

Grill roasting means grilling foods over enclosed indirect or direct heat at lower temperatures than grilling, but higher than barbecuing—usually 300°F to 375°F. The result is more smoky flavor than grilling, but less than barbecuing. Grill roasting is best for large tender cuts of meat that do not need long slow cooking but benefit from developing more smoky flavor, such as pork ribs, lamb racks, whole birds, whole fish, or pork loin.

Spit-roasting or **Rotisserie cooking** involves grilling over direct heat using a rotating skewer, allowing the food to baste itself. The heat source is placed to one side or underneath the food being cooked. On most modern grills or rotisseries, the skewer is motorized. Spit-roasting is becoming a more and more popular way to grill.

Smoking or **Curing.** For centuries (long before refrigeration) foods have been preserved as well as flavored with smoke. The technique uses indirect heat at low temperatures in an enclosed container; sometimes, water is placed inside the container to provide moisture. Temperatures range from 70°F to 85°F for "cold" smoking and 100°F to 200°F for "hot" smoking. Because of the low temperatures, smoking can take a long time—up to 10 hours, for example, for a ham or turkey. Foods can be smoked in a kettle grill, but the temperature can be difficult to control.

Smoker boxes. If you don't have a barrel smoker, you can turn your grill into a smoker with a metal smoker box. Just add soaked wood chips and place the box in the grill.

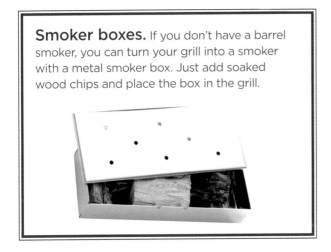

CHOOSING A GRILL

Before buying a grill, answer three questions:
• How often will the grill be used?
• How much space will be dedicated to the grill?
• What kind of fuel you prefer to use in your grill?

Disposable grills. Designed for a single use, a basic disposable grill consists of an aluminum pan with a mesh rack on which to place food. Disposable grills are usually sold with self-lighting charcoal that lasts up to 30 minutes. Their portability makes them ideal for camping and picnics.

Hibachi and **Portable grills.** Usually made of cast iron or steel, hibachis originated in Japan (the word means "firebox"). Their small size makes them convenient for picnics, beach or tailgating parties, camping trips, or whenever you want to grill small amounts of food.

Brazier grills. These open charcoal grills are based on the old-fashioned open-air fires used to roast chestnuts on city streets. Home braziers are a good choice for cooking limited amounts of food in a small space.

Kettle grills. Invented in the United States in the 1950s, the kettle grill is usually three-legged and round, with vents above and below the grilling rack that allow temperature control. Be sure to choose one with a large cooking area and enough space for a hot fire. Grills with deep bowls are better because they allow air to circulate. A tall domed lid gives plenty of space for large items such as roasts and whole birds.

Charcoal ovens. These portable ovens with closeable lids use indirect heat to cook more like an oven than a grill and use smoke to flavor food.

Gas grills. Most gas grills are fueled by a tank of liquid propane and use lava rock or ceramic briquettes set over burners. Gas grills take less time to heat than charcoal grills, their heat level is easier to control and change, and they are less messy than charcoal grills. In addition, gas grills are economical on fuel. Many gas grills have side burners, which can be a real bonus for heating sauces and side dishes.

A GUIDE TO GRILL FUEL AND FLAVORINGS

Wood. Whether you own a wood-burning grill or plan to use chunks or chips, nothing beats the original grill fuel for giving deliciously smoky flavor. Fruit woods such as apple and cherry, and nut woods such as hickory and pecan are best for grilling; maple and oak are also good grilling woods. Mesquite has good flavor but tends to throw out showers of sparks, so it needs careful attention. All these woods burn evenly and at a suitably high temperature, and they burn quickly enough to create a bed of hot coals that is perfect for grilling. None of them is too smoky, and they all impart rich flavor. We recommend fruit woods and maple for poultry and fish, nut woods and mesquite for beef and lamb, and hickory, pecan, maple, and oak for pork. Evergreen woods are too resinous and burn unevenly, so are unsuitable for grilling.

All woods should be aged at least a year or they will be too smoky. Split the wood into lengths about 1 foot long and not too thick (an inch or so). Use newspaper and kindling to get started; wood is ready for cooking when the fire is reduced to glowing embers. Never grill with treated wood, which contains dangerous chemicals.

Wood chips or chunks. You don't need a wood-burning grill to replicate the unique flavor of wood. Wood chips work best for covered grill-roasting or barbecuing; they tend to burn too fast for grilling, but can still provide some flavor. Soak aromatic wood chips or chunks at least 30 minutes before adding to a charcoal fire. It's best not to add too much wood at a time; it will lower the heat significantly or even put out the fire. Instead, add the wood gradually.

Wood chips can also be placed in a smoker box for gas grills. If you do not have a smoker box, you can wrap the wood in heavy-duty foil, poke some small holes in it (to allow the chips to smolder), and place the packet directly over the burners.

Herbs. For extra flavor, consider putting soaked bunches of fresh or dried herbs or spices on the grill fire or in the smoker box. Rosemary sprigs are ideal for lamb and chicken; thyme and sage work well with pork. Juniper berries, fennel, bay leaves, cinnamon sticks, and star anise are other flavorings you might want to try.

Charcoal. Cleaner and more fuel-efficient than fresh or aged wood, charcoal burns hotter than wood or gas, and contributes more flavor than gas grilling. Charcoal will usually burn for 30 to 45 minutes once the fire is ready for grilling before it needs replenishing.

Chimney starters. Usually about 6 inches across, with air vents at the bottom and a heatproof handle, most chimney starters hold 2 pounds of charcoal. To use a chimney starter, place crumpled newspaper in the bottom and add kindling. Fill with the top with charcoal and put the chimney in the center of the fire grate. Open the vents and light the newspaper. After the charcoal has burned for 15 to 20 minutes and is glowing, pour the coals onto the grate. Add charcoal as necessary and wait until the coals are just covered with gray ash. To add charcoal, repeat the process above; when lit, add the charcoal to the fire grate as before.

THE CHARCOAL FIRE

A charcoal fire is built using a couple of layers of briquettes or about 2 inches of lump charcoal. A uniform layer is best for grilling ingredients of similar thickness, such as steaks. For ingredients of varying textures and thicknesses, we recommend preparing a fire with more than one heat level. This can be done by building a single layer of charcoal the whole area, then adding another layer of charcoal over just one other half. The thinner layer will give lower or indirect heat for longer, slower cooking, while the thicker area will provide higher, direct heat for searing. You'll start the cooking on the hotter side, then move it to the cooler part to finish cooking. If you prepare a uniform layer of charcoal, place thicker cuts of meat or vegetables on the hottest part of the grill (usually at the center), and put thinner ones at the edges. As you grill, move the cooked items to the edges until evenly cooked. Bear in mind that it is easier to control and lower the temperature of a hot fire than to revive a cool one, so it's better to use more than you think you might need.

Build the charcoal fire in an area 2 or 3 square inches larger than the food to be cooked, leaving space at the edge of the grill so you can keep food warm without cooking it further. If you have an adjustable fire grate, place it 4 or 5 inches below the cooking grate. This will ensure even medium to medium-high heat. For cooking over high heat, add another layer of charcoal, or reduce the distance between the grates to 2 or 3 inches.

The most efficient way to light a charcoal fire is with a chimney starter (see box, left). You will not need lighter fluid, which many experts feel affects the flavor of the food. Even without lighter fluid, briquettes contain chemicals that must be burned off before you can cook over them. (This is not an issue for lump charcoal.)

ALL ABOUT CHARCOAL

There are two forms of charcoal for grilling:

Lump charcoal. Natural lump charcoal or charwood is derived from mesquite, oak, hickory, or other hardwood that is kiln-fired at very high temperatures with no additives, so the result is all-natural pure carbon. Lump charcoal is completely dry, light in weight, and shaped irregularly, unlike compact briquettes. Although it is more expensive than briquettes, lump charcoal starts more quickly and burns faster and at higher heat, making it particularly good for searing meats. Many experts will tell you that it also smells cleaner than charcoal briquettes.

Charcoal briquettes. Briquettes are made with ground and compressed charcoal, starch, and coal dust. They burn longer and more evenly than lump charcoal, which makes them ideal for indirect grilling. Even if they provide slightly less flavor, as some maintain, briquettes can be used with soaked wood chips to give plenty of smoky tones. Once lit, a briquette fire takes 25 to 30 minutes, on average, to be ready for grilling. Some brands of briquettes contain flammable additives that make them self-igniting, which adds to their convenience. However, because they burn more quickly, they are best mixed with plain briquettes. Another choice that is more expensive but even cleaner and more convenient is self-lighting briquettes in a bag. There is no handling charcoal at all, as you simply light the bag. Note that ceramic briquettes or lava rocks are for use in gas grills only.

If you're using frozen meat or fish or vacuum-sealed foods shipped with dry ice or a freezer pack, it's best to thaw in the sealed package in the refrigerator. Do not thaw at room temperature, as this runs the risk of bacteria formation.

TIMETABLE FOR REFRIGERATOR THAWING

Roast	8 to 15 hours per pound
Steak	16 to 14 hours per pound
Whole Turkey	36 to 48 hours per 4 to 5 pounds
Poultry	24 hours per 1 to 2 pounds

(Small items such as steaks and chops can be thawed quickly in cold water for 30 to 45 minutes. Thaw the food in the sealed packaging.)

You can also light charcoal without a chimney starter. Place crumpled newspaper beneath the fire grate and plenty of kindling on top of the fire grate. Place the charcoal on the kindling and light the newspaper.

A charcoal fire is ready when the coals are glowing (with no flames) and uniformly covered with gray ash, typically 25 to 30 minutes after lighting.

One way to test coals is to spread them out with tongs, replace the cooking grate, and cover the grill. Leave it 5 minutes, then remove the lid and place your hand 4 or 5 inches above the grate. For medium heat, you should be able to hold it there about 5 seconds; medium-high, 3 or 4 seconds; and about 2 seconds for high heat.

If you need more heat at any point, lower the cooking grid, open the vents, or add more charcoal. If the fire is too hot, raise the grid, spread out the coals, open the lid, or close the vents. As a general rule, avoid covering a charcoal grill if possible, unless grill-roasting or barbecuing larger pieces of meat. Smoke, soot, and grease can accumulate on the lid and give the food an unpleasant flavor. Instead, cover food with disposable aluminum pans; they act like mini ovens and retain heat.

FOOD SAFETY TIPS

★ It's ideal to cook foods that have been brought to room temperature (the grill heat can better penetrate and cook the center without burning the exterior); 20 to 30 minutes is usually enough time. Seafood and other highly perishable foods should be refrigerated until cooked.

★ Refrigerate all meats and fish in a sealed storage bag or container on a lower shelf in the refrigerator to prevent leakages and drips. Freeze meat and fish you will not be cooking within 2 or 3 days.

★ Rinse off poultry and fish before cooking. For handling meat and fish safely, never use the same cutting board, work surface, or dishes for raw and cooked ingredients. Thoroughly wash your hands, utensils, cutting boards, and work surfaces that come into contact with raw food with warm soapy water.

★ Do not serve marinades that have been used with raw meat or fish unless you boil them for at least 4 minutes.

GRILLING ACCESSORIES

These days, there is a multitude of accessories for your grill. The good news is that you can usually work with as many or as few as you like! Here is our recommended list of the most important items that will make your grilling experience easier and more successful.

Lighters and matches. A butane trigger lighter is a handy tool for lighting kindling; be sure to choose one with a safety feature so children can't light it. Long fireplace matches are also useful for lighting grills.

Timer. A kitchen timer or clip-on timer will remind you to turn or remove the food from the grill. Digital timers can be set for hours at a time, so are useful for slow cooking and smoking. Wind-up timers work best for cooking times of 60 minutes or less.

Disposable metal pans. A supply of disposable (but reusable) aluminum pans of various sizes can be used as drip trays and for transporting meat and ingredients to and from the grill.

Long-handled stainless-steel spatula. Select a metal spatula (never use a plastic or non-stick spatula, which can melt or burn on the grill). Metal handles can get very hot, so use an oven mitt or select one with a wooden or nonconductive handle. Use a narrower one for steaks and chops; a wide one for whole fish.

Long-handled metal tongs. These allow for maneuvering and turning the food and are preferable to using a fork, which can pierce meat and let the juices escape. Which type you use is up to you; there are flatter versions for grabbing more delicate foods such as chicken breasts and fish, and more clawlike versions that are good for denser foods such as steaks or pork chops. Some have locking handles, which make them easier to store when not in use.

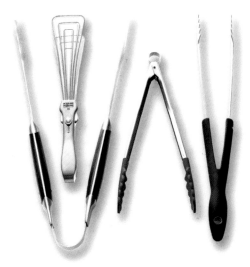

Thermometer. An instant-read thermometer is ideal for steaks and thin cuts of meat. For larger pieces, we recommend a stainless steel meat thermometer with a circular dial. Keep checking the internal temperature of the meat if you want it cooked to the right degree of doneness, and never leave a thermometer in the meat while grilling.

Mitts. Oven mitts and pot holders are a must. Be sure to keep them away from the grill surface so they don't catch on fire. Mitts are a better choice because they cover more of your hands and arms, but pot holders are better than kitchen towels (or worse, nothing).

Spray bottle. Keep a plastic spray bottle of water on hand to damp down flare-ups or for cooling the fire.

Cleaning brush. A long-handled stiff wire brush is a must for easy cleanup. We recommend a rustproof brass brush with a scraper on the end to help remove hardened grease. Cleaning the grill with a brush is easiest when the grill has cooled down a bit but is still somewhat warm.

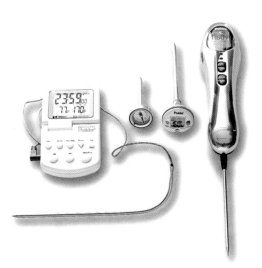

Grilling basket. Grilling small items such as scallops, shrimp, and vegetables is simpler with a grilling basket. They are available with and without handles.

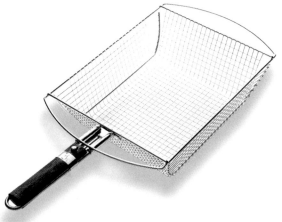

A Grill Timing Guide

Grilling is an inexact science, as so many different factors come into play. Besides type of grill and the size of the fire (not to mention weather conditions and altitude), the exact weight, quality, thickness, and size of the food being grilled are other important issues that affect timing. Cooking times given in recipes are guidelines rather than exact rules, so it is important to test food with a thermometer or by touch (see below) to make sure it is cooked to the desired doneness. Most cuts of meat and fish should be turned just once. Smaller items such as kabobs and sausages should be turned more often to ensure even cooking. We specify grilling for the same amount of time on each side. If you prefer, cook a little longer on the first side (for example, if the total cooking time is 10 to 12 minutes, grill 6 to 7 minutes on the first side and 4 to 5 minutes on the second); the second side will be warming even while it is away from the direct heat. Unless otherwise specified in the recipes, it is best to turn smaller cuts of meat (including steaks and chops) just once.

The charts on the next few pages list recommended cooking times for each stage of doneness. Temperatures shown in the chart reflect fully cooked temperatures and allow for a few minutes of standing time to let the meat juices redistribute internally. At the time you remove meat from the grill, the internal temperature will be 5°F to 10°F lower than those listed because residual heat will cause the temperature of the meat to rise after it has been removed from the heat. (The charts refer to direct heat unless noted.)

THE TOUCH TEST

With roasts or whole birds, an instant-read thermometer is the best way to gauge doneness. For smaller items such as steak and chops, however, you can test doneness by touch.

Rare	Soft to touch; gives to pressure, though not as soft as raw meat.
Medium-rare	Soft and springy to touch. Slowly springs back when pressed.
Medium	Feels somewhat firm, yet spongy; springs back readily when pressed.
Medium-well	Feels firm; springs back readily when pressed.
Well done	Feels firm, does not give to pressure.

Beef. We recommend medium-rare for most cuts of beef. Slow-cooked meats like briskets and ribs will be more cooked, but the low heat and application of liquid keep them from getting dried out. Ground beef should be cooked medium-well or 160°F.

	RARE 130°F	MEDIUM-RARE 140°F	MEDIUM 150°F	MEDIUM-WELL 160°F	
CUT (THICKNESS/WEIGHT)			TOTAL GRILL TIME (MINUTES)		
	RARE	MEDIUM-RARE	MEDIUM	MEDIUM-WELL	WELL
Hamburger (½ inch/8 oz)	NR	NR	NR	14 to 16	18 to 20
Rib-eye (¾ inch/6 oz)	about 4	5 to 6	7 to 8	9 to 10	about 12
Sirloin (1 inch/7 oz)	5 to 6	8 to 9	10 to 12	about 14	15 to 16
Porterhouse (1 inch/1 lb)	7 to 8	10 to 11	12 to 14	about 16	18 to 20
Fillet mignon (1½ inches/7 oz)	7 to 8	10 to 11	12 to 14	about 16	18 to 20
Flank steak (1½ lbs)	7 to 8	10 to 12	14 to 16	about 16	18 to 20
Rib-eye roast** (4 lbs)	45 to 50	60 to 90	90 to 120	100 to 110	about 120

** grilled over medium indirect heat

CUTS OF STEAK

Everyone has different tastes and every steak has its own unique characteristics. Here are six popular cuts that are widely available.

FILLET MIGNON
Actually a piece of the tenderloin, this delicate, lightly marbled cut has the mildest flavor of any cut of beef.

STRIP STEAK
This is a firm, well-marbled steak from the heart of the loin. The characteristic "white tail" keeps it juicy during cooking.

PORTERHOUSE
Often large enough to feed two people, this steak is really two steaks in one. On one side of the bone is a strip loin; on the other is a fillet mignon.

T-BONE
The classic T-Bone is similar to the Porterhouse, except that the T-Bone has a smaller fillet.

RIBEYE
Available both boneless and bone-in, this richly marbled steak is cut directly from the prime rib.

TOP SIRLOIN
This cut has a very "beefy" flavor, which is heightened by the strip of exterior fat that runs along its side.

Pork. We recommend medium to medium-well for most cuts of pork. Slow-cooked meats like roasts and ribs will be more cooked, but the low heat and application of liquid keep them from getting dried out. Ground pork should be cooked to at least 160°F.

CUT	THICKNESS/WEIGHT	MEDIUM 160°F MEDIUM-WELL 170°F TOTAL GRILL TIME (MINUTES)	
		MEDIUM-RARE	MEDIUM
Boneless chop	1 inch/4 oz	NR	8 to 10
Boneless chop	1 inch/8 oz	NR	10 to 12
Loin	12 oz	NR	25 to 30
Spare ribs**	1½-lb rack	NR	60 to 75
Baby back ribs**	1½-lb rack	NR	70 to 80

** grilled over medium indirect heat

Poultry. We recommend that chicken and other poultry be cooked to a minimum of 165°F, with the exception of duck breasts which should be cooked to 150°F. Ground chicken and turkey should be cooked through to an internal temperature of 165°F.

	THICKNESS/WEIGHT	TOTAL GRILL TIME (COOKED THROUGH)
CHICKEN		
Boneless breast	4 oz	10 to 12 minutes
Wings		12 to 15 minutes
Whole**	3 lbs	75 to 80 minutes
Whole**	4 lbs	90 to 95 minutes
TURKEY		
Whole**	12 lbs	About 3 hours
DUCK		
Skinless boneless breast	6 oz	8 minutes (to medium-rare)
Whole**	5 lbs	About 2 hours

** grilled over medium indirect heat

Lamb & Game. We recommend medium-rare to medium for most cuts of lamb and game meats like venison, buffalo, and ostrich. Slow-cooked legs of lamb will be more cooked, but the low heat and application of liquid keep them from getting dried out.

	RARE 130°F	MEDIUM-RARE 140°F	MEDIUM 150°F	MEDIUM-WELL 165°F
		THICKNESS/WEIGHT	TOTAL GRILL TIME (MINUTES)	
			MEDIUM-RARE	MEDIUM
Steaks		3/4 inch/8 oz	6 to 7	8 to 10
Rib chops		1 1/2 inches/6 oz	11 to 12	14 to 16
Rack**		2 lbs	35 to 40	40 to 45
Leg, boneless**		4 lbs	45 to 50	55 to 60
Leg, bone-in**		6 lbs	110 to 120	135

** grilled over medium indirect heat

Seafood. We recommend that fish fillets and steaks (other than tuna) be cooked to a minimum of 145°F; tuna should be cooked to 125°F. Shellfish should be cooked just until opaque.

	THICKNESS/ WEIGHT	TOTAL GRILL TIME (MINUTES) MEDIUM
Fish fillets	1/2 inch	5 to 7
Fish fillets	1 inch	8 to 10
Fish steaks	1 inch	9 to 12
Whole fish**	2 lb	25 to 30
Lobster tails	6 oz	12 to 15
Sea Scallops		2 to 5
Jumbo Shrimp		4 to 6

** grilled over medium indirect heat

Vegetables. Vegetables should be cooked until marked and charred in places, but not completely black (with the exception of peppers and tomatoes when you plan to remove the skin).

	THICKNESS/ WEIGHT	TOTAL GRILL TIME (MINUTES)
Asparagus	Thin/thick	3 to 4/6 to 8
Corn	Whole ear	8 to 10
Corn**	Whole ear	12 to 15
Eggplant	Sliced	12 to 15
Mushrooms	Button	7 to 8
Mushrooms	Portobello	10 to 12
Onions	Sliced	6 to 8
Bell peppers	Whole	12 to 15 (charred)
Squash	Sliced	8 to 10
Tomatoes	Whole	10 to 12 (charred)

** grilled over medium indirect heat

A Grill Safety Guide

The smoky flavor and charring produced by grilling cannot be duplicated through any other cooking method. And while we never want to sacrifice taste, being safe is the first and most important step to take when cooking with fire.

★ Place the grill on a level surface and make sure it is well ventilated. Do not move the grill once it is lit.

★ Unless you have a properly vented electric or gas grill, never grill in an enclosed area, as it creates a potential fire hazard. It may also cause breathing problems or smoke damage, or create potentially lethal carbon monoxide fumes.

★ Keep the grill away from anything combustible. Keep the grill several feet away from walls, deck railings, utility poles, etc.

★ Avoid grilling over charcoal when it is windy. Sparks and embers can be blown around.

★ Before using a grill for the first time, carefully read the manufacturer's instructions, paying special attention to warning labels, safety information, and fuel recommendations.

★ Keep the fire under control at all times, especially when lighting charcoal with lighter fluid.

★ When grilling with charcoal, use only lighter fluid. Never use gasoline, alcohol, kerosene, or any other flammable substance, as they are volatile and can cause burns or even explode. Do not add lighter fluid to hot (or even warm) charcoal.

★ Never leave a grill unattended.

★ Leave no more than a quarter inch of fat on meat. Fat dripping onto hot coals can cause flare-ups.

★ Before lighting the grill, oil the grid lightly to prevent foods from sticking, especially lean foods such as fish or vegetables. Use cooking oil and a cloth or nonstick cooking spray. Do not oil the grill once the fire is started. You can also lightly brush oil on the food before placing it on the grill.

★ Take care when opening the cover of a grill or barbecue; steam and smoke can cause injuries. Use an oven mitt to avoid burns.

★ For charcoal grills, keep a dry-spray extinguisher on hand in case of serious flare-ups.

★ Keep a first-aid kit handy. Treat minor burns by holding the affected area under cold running water. Seek medical attention for more serious burns.

★ Be sure to extinguish or turn off the grill after use. For charcoal fires, the most effective method is to close all the vents and to cover the grill tightly with the lid. Do not remove any coals until they are completely cold.

★ With gas grills, if you smell gas, do not light the grill. Always light a gas grill with the cover up and the burners turned to the ignition setting or to high. If the grill still does not light, wait 2 or 3 minutes before trying again to allow the gas to dissipate.

★ Store gas tanks upright in an open but shady outside space. Never keep them in an enclosed area in case of leakage or explosion.

Rubs, Sauces and Marinades

Brandied Cracked Pepper

This is a wonderful coating for grilled steaks. It also works as a seasoning for hamburgers, poultry, and game.

PREP TIME: 5 mins ★ MAKES about 2 cups

2 cups (8 ounces) cracked black pepper
2 tablespoons dried orange peel
1 cup brandy

1 Combine the pepper and orange peel in a shallow 9x13-inch baking pan. Pour in the brandy and toss to blend.

2 Cover lightly with plastic wrap and set aside 2 days, or until the pepper mix has absorbed all of the brandy.

3 Transfer to an airtight container and store in a cool, dry spot up to 6 months.

Sweet Spice Rub

You can vary the amount of chile powder to suit your tolerance for spiciness. The pure red chile powder used in this recipe is not the same thing as "chili" powder, which is less spicy and contains ground dried chiles, seasonings, and salt.

PREP TIME: 10 mins ★ MAKES about 1/2 cup

1 Combine all ingredients in a small bowl and mix thoroughly.

2 Use immediately or transfer to an airtight container and store in a cool, dry spot up to 6 months.

> 1/2 cup pure red chile powder
> 2 tablespoons brown sugar
> 1 tablespoon sweet paprika
> 2 teaspoons ground cumin
> 2 teaspoons coarse salt

Savory Spice Rub

The spices in this rub add a complex flavor to meat such as pork or lamb. For those more sensitive to spicy heat, consider easing up on the amount of chile powder.

PREP TIME: 10 mins ★ MAKES about 11/2 cups

1 Combine all ingredients in a small bowl and mix thoroughly.

2 Transfer to an airtight container, cover, and store in a cool, dry spot up to 6 months.

> 1/2 cup pure red chile powder
> 1/2 cup sweet paprika
> 1/2 cup ground coriander
> 1/2 cup ground cumin
> 1/2 cup fennel seeds, crushed
> 1/2 cup celery seeds, crushed
> 1 tablespoon ground cardamom
> 1 tablespoon garlic salt
> 1 tablespoon black pepper

Sweet Spice Rub (left)
Savory Spice Rub (right)

Spicy Red Wine Marinade

This is a terrific marinade for all types of beef, game, duck, and even chicken.

PREP TIME: 10 mins ★ MAKES about 3 cups

2 cups fruity red wine (such as Zinfandel)
1/2 cup balsamic vinegar
1/2 cup red wine vinegar
8 cloves
8 allspice berries
2 cloves garlic, peeled and smashed
1 onion, sliced
1 teaspoon cracked black pepper
Dried red pepper flakes (optional)

1 Combine the wine with the balsamic and red wine vinegars in a small nonreactive container. Add the cloves, allspice berries, garlic, onion, cracked pepper, and the red pepper flakes, if using. Stir to blend.

2 Place the item to be marinated in a shallow glass baking dish. Pour the marinade over the top, cover, and refrigerate, turning occasionally, at least 1 hour or longer, depending upon the type of meat used. If not using immediately, cover and refrigerate up to 3 days. Lighter meats should be marinated only an hour or so; rich meats, such as game, can stand in the marinade up to 12 hours.

Apple-Maple Marinade

This sweet marinade is reminiscent of fall in New England—freshly picked apples and pancakes with local maple syrup. It gives that same feeling to poultry, pork, duck, and winter vegetables.

PREP TIME: 10 mins ★ MAKES about 4 1/2 cups

2 cups apple cider
1 cup apple cider vinegar
1 cup pure maple syrup
3 tablespoons peanut oil
2 tablespoons freshly squeezed lemon juice
2 tablespoons chopped fresh sage
1 tablespoon chopped fresh flat-leaf parsley
2 teaspoons freshly grated lemon zest

1 Combine the cider, vinegar, syrup, oil, and lemon juice in a small nonreactive container. Stir in the sage, parsley, and zest.

2 Place the item to be marinated in a shallow glass baking dish. Pour the marinade over, cover, and refrigerate, turning occasionally, for at least 2 hours or up to 4 hours. If not using immediately, cover and refrigerate for up to 3 days.

Tequila Sunrise Marinade

Spicy and slightly sweet, this is a wonderful marinade for shrimp, chicken, pork, and thick fish steaks, like salmon or swordfish. It can also be used as a dipping sauce for kabobs or grilled shellfish.

PREP TIME: 15 mins ★ MAKES about 3 cups

1 Combine the orange, lime, and cranberry juices with the tequila, peanut oil, and liqueur in a small nonreactive bowl, stirring to blend well. Stir in the serrano and cilantro.

2 Place the item to be marinated in a medium shallow glass baking dish. Pour the marinade over, cover, and refrigerate, turning occasionally, at least 1 hour or up to 3 hours. If not using immediately, cover and refrigerate up to 3 days.

1 cup freshly squeezed orange juice

1/2 cup freshly squeezed lime juice

1/2 cup cranberry juice

1/2 cup tequila

1/2 cup peanut oil

1 tablespoon orange-flavored liqueur, such as triple sec

1 serrano chile, seeded and chopped, or to taste

2 tablespoons chopped fresh cilantro

Jet-Fresh Pineapple Sauce

Look for "jet-fresh" pineapples at your grocery or specialty store—these are fresh, sweet Hawaiian pineapples that yield plenty of tropical flavor.

PREP TIME: **10 mins** ★ COOK TIME: **20 mins** ★ MAKES about 1½ cups

1 pineapple, peeled, cored, and chopped

½ cup chopped onion

2 red serrano or jalapeño chiles, seeded and minced

½ cup freshly squeezed lime juice

1 Place all the ingredients in a blender and puree. Transfer to a saucepan and bring to a simmer over medium heat. Reduce the heat to low and cook 10 minutes, or until thickened. Serve warm.

2 If not using immediately, transfer to an airtight container, cover, and store, refrigerated, up to 3 days.

Herb-Mustard Marinade

This aromatic marinade is perfect for shellfish, fish, chicken, or pork. Fish should marinate no more than 30 minutes while meats can marinate for up to 2 hours.

PREP TIME: 20 mins ★ MAKES about 2 cups

1 Combine the wine and vinegar with the shallots, fennel, mustard, and garlic in a small nonreactive container, stirring to blend well. Add the herbs, stirring to combine.

2 Place the item to be marinated in a shallow glass baking dish. Pour the marinade over the top, cover, and refrigerate, turning occasionally at least 30 minutes or up to 2 hours, depending upon the type of food being marinated. If not using immediately, cover and refrigerate up to 3 days.

> 1 cup dry rosé wine
> ½ cup raspberry or white wine vinegar
> ½ cup minced shallots
> ½ cup minced fennel bulb
> 2 tablespoons grainy Dijon mustard
> 1 teaspoon minced garlic
> 1 tablespoon each chopped fresh rosemary, thyme, flat-leaf parsley, and basil

Mango-Chile Sauce

This fruity sauce has a pleasing kick that will wake up your taste buds and perfectly complement grilled chicken, pork, and many kinds of firm-fleshed, non-oily fish.

COOK TIME: 15 mins ★ MAKES about 2½ cups

1 Place all the ingredients in a saucepan and bring to a boil. Turn down the heat to medium-low and simmer, uncovered, 15 minutes or until the sauce has thickened a little. Keep warm.

2 If not using immediately, transfer to an airtight container, cover, and store, refrigerated, up to 3 days.

> 2 cups mango nectar or mango puree (thawed if frozen)
> ½ cup vegetable broth or chicken broth
> ½ cup white wine vinegar
> ½ tablespoon hot pepper sauce
> ½ teaspoon coarse salt

Original Barbecue Sauce

This classic sauce is perfect for ribs, chicken, burgers, and hot dogs. If you prefer, the beer can be replaced with orange juice, the syrup with honey, and the salt with soy sauce.

PREP TIME: **5 mins** ★ COOK TIME: **50 mins** ★ MAKES **about 6 cups**

2 tablespoons peanut oil
1 cup minced onion
1 tablespoon minced garlic
3 cups tomato ketchup
1 cup dark beer
1/2 cup apple cider vinegar
1/2 cup light brown sugar
3 tablespoons Worcestershire sauce
2 tablespoons pure maple syrup
2 tablespoons pure red chile powder
2 teaspoons dry mustard
Hot pepper sauce
Salt and pepper

1 Heat the oil in a large heavy saucepan over medium heat. Add the onion and garlic. Cook, stirring frequently, 5 minutes or until very soft and beginning to take on some color. Add the ketchup, beer, vinegar, brown sugar, Worcestershire sauce, maple syrup, chile powder, and mustard, stirring to blend. Season with hot pepper sauce, salt, and pepper to taste and cook, stirring frequently, about 45 minutes or until the sauce is thick and the flavors are well blended.

2 Remove from the heat. If not using immediately, transfer to an airtight container, cover, and store, refrigerated, up to 2 weeks.

Moppin' Sauce

This sauce can be brushed on while grilling or used as a marinade or cooking sauce for pork, ribs, chicken, game, or even winter squash.

PREP TIME: **5 mins** ★ COOK TIME: **30 mins** ★ MAKES **about 3½ cups**

1 cup tomato ketchup
1/2 cup applesauce
1/2 cup bourbon
1/2 cup apple juice
1/2 cup Dijon mustard
1/2 cup honey
1 teaspoon minced garlic
Celery salt
Hot pepper sauce
Salt and pepper

1 Combine the ketchup, applesauce, bourbon, apple juice, mustard, honey, and garlic in a medium saucepan over medium heat. Season with celery salt, hot pepper sauce, salt, and pepper to taste and cook, stirring frequently, about 30 minutes or until the sauce is thick and the flavors have blended.

2 Remove from the heat and, if not using immediately, transfer to an airtight container, cover, and refrigerate up to 1 month.

Chunky BBQ Sauce

Chunks of pineapple and onion make this hearty sauce even more satisfying and tasty.

PREP TIME: 15 mins ★ COOK TIME: 5 mins ★ MAKES about 2 cups

Combine the pineapple, onion, brown sugar, and vinegar in small saucepan. Cook over high heat 2 to 3 minutes or until liquid is syrupy, stirring occasionally. Reduce heat to medium; add barbecue sauce. Cook and stir about 1 minute or until heated through. Serve warm.

> 1/4 cup drained canned pineapple chunks, coarsely chopped
> 1/4 cup chopped red onion
> 1 tablespoon packed brown sugar
> 1 1/2 teaspoons balsamic vinegar
> 1/2 cup prepared mild barbecue sauce

Starters and Light Meals

Grilled Eggplant-Tomato Pizza

Grilling gives pizzas a flavor dimension that you will want to experience again and again. To make this pizza in a hurry, use packaged refrigerated pizza dough.

PREP TIME: 2 hours 15 minutes ★ GRILL TIME: 35 mins ★ SERVES 4

For the Pizza Dough:

½ cup lukewarm water (110°F)

1 package active dry yeast

1 tablespoon honey

2 cups all-purpose flour, plus more as needed

½ teaspoon coarse salt

2 tablespoons olive oil

For the Pizza Topping:

1 eggplant, about 1 pound, cut crosswise into ½-inch slices

2 teaspoons coarse salt

2 cups cherry tomatoes, quartered

3 cloves garlic, minced

½ cup olive oil, divided

1 cup (4 ounces) shredded mozzarella cheese

1 cup fresh basil leaves, minced

2 tablespoons freshly Parmesan cheese

1 For the Dough, pour the water into a small bowl and sprinkle the yeast over it. Whisk in the honey; let sit in a warm place 5 minutes. Sift the flour and salt into a large bowl. Stir in the yeast mixture and mix until a soft dough forms. Add the oil and mix until the dough becomes shiny and forms a ball. Turn the dough out onto a lightly floured work surface and knead 7 to 8 minutes or until smooth. Add more flour as needed.

2 Transfer the dough to a lightly oiled medium bowl and cover with plastic wrap. Let rise in a warm place 45 minutes to 1 hour or until doubled in volume. Return dough to a lightly floured work surface and divide into 4 portions. Knead each portion for 1 minute and form into balls. Place on a baking sheet, cover, and let rise for 20 minutes. Roll each ball into a 6-inch round about ⅛ inch thick, sprinkling the dough and rolling pin with flour to prevent them from sticking. Pinch the edges of the dough to create a raised edge. Set aside. Preheat and oil the grill.

3 For the Topping, place the eggplant in a colander and sprinkle with 1 teaspoon coarse salt. Let drain 20 minutes, turning slices after 10 minutes. Combine the tomatoes and garlic in a medium bowl and toss to mix. Set aside.

4 Transfer the eggplant to a work surface and pat dry with paper towels. Brush with 3 tablespoons of the olive oil and grill over direct medium heat 7 to 8 minutes, turning once, until tender and cooked through. Remove from the grill, cut the slices in half, and set aside.

5 Grill the dough over direct high heat, covered, for about 1 minute or until the bottom is firm and lightly marked. Remove from the grill and brush the grilled side of the pizza with the remaining 1 tablespoon olive oil. Top each pizza with about one fourth of the grilled eggplant and tomato mixture and sprinkle with mozzarella. Return to the grill, cover, and grill over direct heat for 3 to 4 minutes or until the cheese has melted. Repeat with remaining dough and topping. Garnish with the basil and sprinkle with the Parmesan. Cut into wedges and serve hot.

Steakhouse Crostini

This hearty starter is simple enough to whip up on short notice, but elegant enough to serve to company. Use a whole-grain or sourdough baguette for the toasts, if you like.

PREP TIME: 30 mins ★ GRILL TIME: 3 mins ★ SERVES 8

1 Preheat and oil the grill to medium-high. Preheat the oven to 450°F. Grill the tenderloin pieces over direct medium-high heat, turning the meat so that all sides get browned and cooked to the desired doneness, about 2 or 3 minutes for medium-rare and 3 to 4 minutes for medium. Dice tenderloin into ½-inch cubes. Transfer to a small bowl and stir in the mushroom tapenade. Set aside.

2 Stir together the steak sauce and cream cheese until smooth and creamy.

3 Spread each baguette slice with 1 teaspoon of the cream cheese mixture. Top each with 1 heaping tablespoon of the steak mixture; sprinkle each with 1 tablespoon of crumbled feta. Place on a baking sheet and bake for 5 minutes. Garnish with diced roasted red peppers and chopped Italian parsley. Serve warm.

1 pound tenderloin pieces, cut into 2-inch chunks

½ cup prepared mushroom tapenade

¼ cup prepared steak sauce

8 ounces cream cheese, softened

1 baguette, sliced on the bias into 16 slices and toasted

4 ounces crumbled feta cheese

3 roasted red peppers, diced for garnish

Chopped Italian parsley leaves, for garnish

Warm Shrimp Cocktail

Here's a new twist on shrimp cocktail. Switch it up even more and serve the warm shrimp over a mixed green salad and pour the sauce over all.

PREP TIME: 20 mins ★ GRILL TIME: 5 mins ★ SERVES 4

For the Shrimp:

1 cup dry white wine

2 tablespoons extra-virgin olive oil

1 tablespoon fresh lemon juice

1 teaspoon hot pepper sauce

1 teaspoon minced fresh flat-leaf parsley

16 jumbo shrimp, peeled and deveined

Salt and pepper

For the Cocktail Sauce:

1 cup bottled chili sauce

2 tablespoons bottled horseradish, well drained

1 tablespoon fresh lemon juice

1 teaspoon hot pepper sauce or to taste

½ teaspoon Worcestershire sauce

Lemon wedges, for garnish

1 **For the Shrimp**, whisk together the wine, olive oil, lemon juice, hot pepper sauce, and parsley in a small bowl.

2 Thread 4 shrimp onto each of 4 skewers. Place the skewers in a shallow dish and pour the marinade over. Turn the shrimp to coat, cover with plastic wrap, and refrigerate 1 hour or up to 4 hours. Meanwhile, prepare the cocktail sauce.

3 **For the Cocktail Sauce**, combine all ingredients in a small bowl and stir until blended. If not using immediately, cover and refrigerate up to 5 days.

4 Preheat and oil the grill. Remove the skewers from the marinade and season with salt and pepper to taste. Place the skewers on the grill and grill over direct medium-high heat, turning occasionally, about 4 minutes or until the shrimp are nicely charred and cooked through. Remove from the heat and gently push the shrimp off of the skewers.

5 Arrange 4 shrimp on each of 4 plates. Garnish with lemon wedges. Serve warm with Cocktail Sauce on the side.

Top Sirloin Satay

Satay are a classic Thai appetizer and a big hit at parties everywhere.

PREP TIME: 15 mins ★ GRILL TIME: 10 mins ★ SERVES 6 (3 satay each)

1 **For the Satay,** whisk together the teriyaki sauce, garlic, ginger, sugar, and salt until blended. Add the sirloin strips and toss to coat. Refrigerate at least 2 hours and up to 4 hours.

2 Cover 18 bamboo skewers with water and let them soak at least 2 hours.

3 **For the Peanut Sauce,** combine all ingredients except the cilantro and peanuts in a small bowl and mix until blended. Refrigerate until serving.

4 Preheat and oil the grill to medium-high. Remove the beef strips from the marinade; discard marinade. Thread a piece of beef onto each skewer, running the skewer through each strip twice to hold the strip on the skewer. Working in three batches, grill the skewers over direct medium-high heat 30 seconds to 1 minute on each side for medium-rare. Garnish with chopped cilantro and peanuts. Serve with Peanut Sauce on the side.

For the Satay:

1 cup prepared teriyaki sauce

1 tablespoon chopped garlic

1 tablespoon minced fresh ginger

1 tablespoon packed light brown sugar

1 teaspoon coarse salt

6 sirloin steaks (about 5 ounces each), cut against the grain into 18 thin strips

For the Peanut Sauce:

1/2 cup unsweetened coconut milk

1/3 cup creamy peanut butter

1 tablespoon peeled and minced fresh ginger

1 tablespoon soy sauce

1 tablespoon freshly squeezed lime juice

2 teaspoons toasted (dark) sesame oil

1 teaspoon packed light brown sugar

1/2 teaspoon coarse salt

1/4 teaspoon cayenne pepper

2 tablespoons finely chopped fresh cilantro, for garnish

1 tablespoon toasted peanuts, chopped, for garnish

Chef's Tip: Chicken Satay

Make the Peanut Sauce as above, doubling the recipe. Cut 3 boneless, skinless chicken breasts lengthwise into 18 strips. Place in a glass baking dish and cover with half of the Peanut Sauce. Cover and refrigerate 1 hour. Preheat and oil the grill. Thread a chicken strip onto each skewer, running the skewer through each strip at least twice to hold the strip securely. Grill over direct medium-high heat, turning frequently, about 8 minutes or until the chicken is cooked through. Garnish with peanuts and cilantro. Serve hot with the remaining Peanut Sauce.

Cocktail Chicken Kabobs

Decorative cocktail picks make these kabobs look inviting on any serving tray.

PREP TIME: 10 mins ★ GRILL TIME: 4 mins ★ SERVES 4 to 6

1 whole boneless, skinless chicken breast (about 1 pound) cut into 24 ½-inch cubes

½ cup freshly squeezed orange juice

½ cup freshly squeezed lime juice

1 tablespoon peanut oil

1 teaspoon light brown sugar

1 teaspoon hoisin sauce

1 clove garlic, minced

Cayenne pepper

Coarse salt

24 fresh cilantro leaves

24 cocktail onions, well drained and patted dry for garnish

Prepared duck sauce, for serving

1 Combine the orange juice and lime juice with the oil, sugar in a glass baking dish, stirring to dissolve. Add the garlic, cayenne, and salt. Add the chicken, turn to coat, and cover with plastic wrap. Refrigerate 30 minutes. Preheat and oil the grill.

2 Remove the chicken pieces from the marinade. Place a perforated grill rack on the grill. Lay the chicken pieces in a single layer on the rack and grill over direct medium-high heat, turning frequently, about 4 minutes or until cooked through and glazed slightly. Remove from the grill.

3 With a decorated cocktail pick, stab a cilantro leaf near its base so it lays flat. Then add an onion and a piece of chicken. Repeat with remaining picks, cilantro, onions, and chicken. Serve warm with duck sauce on the side.

Chef's Tip: Kabob Variations

We have used little cocktail onions to complete these kabobs, but you can use almost anything—a small piece of fruit (pineapple, mango, and papaya work particularly well), a small cube of cooked vegetable, or a lightly steamed snow pea pod. You can also marinate the fruit or vegetable with the chicken for extra flavor. If you do marinate other ingredients with the chicken, build the kabobs completely and cook the chicken and the other ingredients together.

Hellzapoppin' Wings

You can make this version of the football-watching favorite as hot as you like.

PREP TIME: 15 mins ★ GRILL TIME: 25 mins ★ SERVES 4

1 For the Dressing, combine the sour cream, blue cheese, mayonnaise, and vinegar in a blender. Process until smooth and season with salt and pepper to taste. Transfer to a serving bowl and stir in the chives. Cover with plastic wrap and refrigerate until serving.

2 For the Wings, preheat and oil the grill. Place the wings in a shallow baking dish. Combine the jelly, hot pepper sauce, mustard, and paprika in a small saucepan over medium heat. Cook, stirring, about 3 minutes or until the jelly has melted and the mustard and paprika are blended. Season with salt and pepper to taste. Remove from the heat and pour over the wings, tossing to coat well.

**3 Grill the wings, turning frequently, about 25 minutes or until cooked through and nicely charred. Remove from the grill. Serve hot with the dressing on the side.

For the Blue Cheese Dressing:
1/2 cup sour cream
4 ounces crumbled blue cheese
1/2 cup mayonnaise
3 tablespoons white wine vinegar
Salt and pepper
2 tablespoons chopped chives

For the Wings:
3 dozen chicken wings, separated at the joint
1 cup sweet pepper jelly
2 tablespoons hot pepper sauce, or to taste
1 teaspoon dry mustard
1 teaspoon paprika
Salt and pepper

Grilled Steak and Corn Soup

During the fall and winter months, there is nothing quite as satisfying as a bowl of this hearty steak soup. For even more flavor, season the steak before grilling with one of the spice rubs on pages 22 and 23. Serve with warm flour tortillas.

PREP TIME: 50 mins ★ COOK TIME: 50 mins ★ GRILL TIME: 18 mins ★ SERVES 4

2 top sirloin steaks, about 8 ounces each and 1⅛-inch thick), or 1 pound flank steak

Salt and pepper

1 red bell pepper, cut in half and seeded

1 yellow bell pepper, cut in half and seeded

1 jalapeño pepper

3 tablespoons olive oil

1 onion, diced

2 large cloves garlic, minced

1 cup diced celery

1 cup peeled and diced carrot

2 tablespoons all-purpose flour

½ teaspoon ground cumin

½ teaspoon dried oregano

6 cups beef broth

1 can (14 ounces) diced tomatoes

1 cup fresh or frozen corn kernels

1 tablespoon Worcestershire sauce

Tabasco sauce

1 Preheat and oil the grill. Season the steak with salt and pepper to taste and bring to room temperature. Grill over direct medium-high heat 4 minutes per side for medium-rare. Remove from the grill. Let cool and cut into cubes.

2 Brush the bell peppers and jalapeño with 1 tablespoon olive oil and grill over direct medium heat 8 to 10 minutes, turning occasionally. Remove from the grill and when cool, remove the charred skin of the tomatoes and bell peppers and discard. Cut the jalapeño in half lengthwise, remove the seeds, and mince.

3 Heat the remaining 2 tablespoons of the oil in a large saucepan over medium-high heat. Add the onion, garlic, celery, and carrot. Sauté 7 to 8 minutes or until soft.

4 Sprinkle in the flour, cumin, and oregano, and stir 1 minute. Add the broth and tomatoes. Bring to a simmer. Reduce the heat to low and continue cooking 15 minutes. Stir in the corn, Worcestershire sauce, and Tabasco sauce to taste. Add the steak and peppers and cook 5 minutes longer. Serve hot.

Grilled Tomato Soup

This is not your grandmother's cream of tomato soup!

PREP TIME: 20 mins ★ GRILL TIME: 20 mins ★ SERVES 4

1 Preheat and oil the grill. Grill the tomatoes and bell pepper over indirect medium heat 15 to 20 minutes, until blackened and soft, gently turning occasionally. Remove and let cool.

2 Heat the olive oil in large skillet over medium heat. Add the onion, carrot, celery, and garlic. Cook 8 to 10 minutes until soft. Remove the charred skin of the tomatoes and bell pepper and discard. Roughly chop and add to the onion mixture. Add the broth, sundried tomatoes, and brown sugar. Working in batches if necessary, transfer the mixture to a blender. Puree and transfer to a large saucepan. Bring to a simmer over medium heat, season with salt and pepper to taste, and keep warm.

3 Heat the vinegar in a small saucepan over medium-high heat. Boil until reduced to about 2 tablespoons; the syrup should be thick enough to coat the back of a spoon. Ladle the soup into bowls. Drizzle each serving with about 1 teaspoon of the balsamic syrup. Sprinkle with chopped basil and serve.

1 pound ripe plum tomatoes, halved

1 red bell pepper, halved and seeded

2 tablespoons extra-virgin olive oil

1 onion, chopped

1 carrot, peeled and chopped

1 rib celery, chopped

2 cloves garlic, chopped

2 cups chicken broth

1/2 cup chopped drained oil-packed sun-dried tomatoes

1 teaspoon brown sugar

Salt and pepper

1/2 cup balsamic vinegar

Chopped fresh basil leaves, for garnish

Meat and Game

Sweet Spice-Rubbed Rib-Eyes ★ 42

Smoky Steaks with Chunky BBQ Sauce ★ 43

Double Porterhouse with Roasted Garlic ★ 44

Double Porterhouse with
Blue Cheese–Tomato Butter ★ 45

Pepper-Crusted Beef Tenderloin
with Black Bean–Mango Salsa ★ 46

Filet Mignon with Compound Butter ★ 47

Filet Mignon with Caper Sauce ★ 48

Santa Fe Grilled Rib-Eyes and Corn ★ 49

Mustard-Glazed Top Sirloin ★ 50

Chipotle-Glazed Strip Steaks ★ 50

Grilled Fajitas ★ 52

Grilled Spiced Flank Steak ★ 53

Honey-Glazed Beef Brisket ★ 54

London Broil with Grilled Mushrooms ★ 56

Orange-Flavored Beef Ribs ★ 57

Traditional Chophouse Mixed Grill ★ 58

"Ranchero" Beef Salad ★ 59

Beefstro Salad ★ 60

Beef Tenderloin Sandwich with
Avocado and Black Beans ★ 61

New York Strip BLT Sandwich ★ 62

New York–Style Hot Dogs ★ 63

Citrus-Sage Veal Chops ★ 64

Veal Chops with Sweet and
Sour Onions ★ 65

Pork Tenderloin with
Sesame Marinade ★ 66

Apple-Spice Marinated Pork Loin ★ 68

Glazed Pork Medallions ★ 69.

Country-Style Barbecued Ribs ★ 70

Spice-Rubbed Baby Back Ribs ★ 71

Kentucky Jack–Glazed Pork Chops ★ 72

Jerked Pork Chops ★ 73

Butterflied Leg of Lamb with
Eggplant Compote ★ 75

Leg of Lamb with Tomato-Ginger Sauce ★ 76

Fennel-Dusted Lamb Chops
with Garlic Glaze ★ 77

Mint-Glazed Lamb Chops with
Mint-Cucumber Sauce ★ 78

Yogurt-Marinated Grilled Lamb Chops ★ 79

Pecan-Crusted Rack of Lamb ★ 80

Southwest-Style Buffalo Steaks
with Green Chile Sauce ★ 82

Mustard-Marinated Rabbit ★ 83

Sweet Spice-Rubbed Rib-Eyes

*Juicy, flavorful rib-eye steaks are many people's favorites,
and the sweet and spicy rub shows them off to best advantage.*

PREP TIME: 5 mins ★ GRILL TIME: 10 mins ★ SERVES 4

4 rib-eye steaks, about
   8 ounces each and about
   1 inch thick
1 recipe Sweet Spice Rub
   (page 23)
Olive oil

1 Preheat and oil the grill. Bring the steaks to room temperature.

2 Press spice rub onto both sides of each steak.

3 Grill the steaks over direct medium-high heat 4 to 5 minutes on each side for medium-rare, about 6 minutes per side for medium, or to desired doneness. Remove from the grill and let rest a few minutes before serving.

Chef's Tip: How to "Rub" a Steak
Gently pat both sides of the steak dry with a paper towel. Scoop a generous amount of rub onto the top of the steak and, using your fingers, spread into an even layer about 1/8 inch thick. (The layer should be thick enough to coat the meat but not so heavy that it all falls off when you grill the steak.) Flip the steak and repeat. Dry rubs should be applied just before grilling; otherwise they will begin to absorb moisture from the steak and will not char as well.

Smoky Steaks with Chunky BBQ Sauce

The combination of the spicy rub and wood smoke gives these steaks their unique flavor.

PREP TIME: 10 mins ★ GRILL TIME: 20 mins ★ SERVES 4

1 Preheat and oil the grill. Tear a piece of heavy-duty aluminum foil into a 12-inch square. Place 1 cup dry wood chips onto foil. Fold foil over to cover chips, then fold edge 3 times, pressing each fold firmly to seal. Fold sides in 3 times, pressing each fold firmly to seal.

2 Press spice rub onto steaks (see page 42 for how-to).

3 Place foil packet directly on the medium coals (place it to one side, not in the center). Grill steaks in the center of the grid (not directly over foil packet) 10 minutes per side for medium-rare, or 12 minutes per side for medium.

4 Remove the steak from the grill, place on a serving platter, and let stand a few minutes. Meanwhile, heat sauce. Slice steaks, season with salt to taste, and serve.

> 2 T-bone steaks, about 12 ounces each and about 1 inch thick
>
> 4 tablespoons Savory Spice Rub (page 23)
>
> 2 cups Chunky BBQ Sauce (page 29), for serving
>
> Salt

Double Porterhouse with Roasted Garlic

A porterhouse has a larger section of tenderloin than a T-bone. One porterhouse will usually feed 4 people. The sweetness of roasted garlic adds just the right touch to this easy-to-prepare dinner.

PREP TIME: **5 mins** ★ COOK TIME: **30 mins** ★ GRILL TIME: **25 mins** ★ SERVES **4**

1 porterhouse steak, 3½ to
  4 pounds and 2 inches thick
  (or 4 steaks, about 16 ounces
  each and 1 inch thick)
4 whole heads garlic
½ cup olive oil
Salt and pepper

1 Preheat the oven to 350°F. Preheat and oil the grill. Bring the steak to room temperature.

2 Cut each head of garlic crosswise, removing just the very top. Place the heads on a piece of aluminum foil. Drizzle with olive oil and season with salt and pepper to taste. Tightly close the foil. Bake for about 30 minutes or until the garlic flesh is very soft and sweet. Remove from the oven and set aside.

3 Meanwhile, fold the tail of the steak back toward the body and use a metal skewer to hold it securely. Season with salt and pepper to taste.

4 Grill over direct medium-high heat for 12 minutes on each side for medium-rare, 14 to 15 minutes on each side for medium. (Cook 1-inch-thick steaks 10 minutes on each side for medium-rare or 12 minutes for medium.)

5 Remove the steak from the grill, place on a serving platter, and let rest for a few minutes. Place the roasted garlic heads on the platter and serve, carving the steak at the table. Garnish each serving with a whole head of garlic.

Double Porterhouse with Blue Cheese–Tomato Butter

This recipe makes more butter than you'll need. Try it on garlic bread or a baked potato.

PREP TIME: 15 mins ★ COOK TIME: 5 mins ★ GRILL TIME: 25 mins ★ SERVES 4

1 For the Butter, heat olive oil over medium heat. Add garlic to pan and cook until golden.

2 Add sun-dried tomatoes to pan; cook 1 minute. Remove the pan from the heat and stir in lemon juice, Worcestershire sauce, and basil. Transfer the mixture to a food processor or blender. Add blue cheese and puree until blended. Add butter and puree until blended and smooth.

3 Transfer mixture to a sheet of plastic wrap. Roll into a log about 1½ inch thick and twist the ends to close. Refrigerate at least 4 hours and up to overnight. Remove from the refrigerator and slice into ½-inch coins when the steaks go on the grill.

4 For the Porterhouse, preheat and oil the grill. Bring the steak to room temperature. Fold the tail of the steak back toward the body and use a metal skewer to hold it securely. Season with salt and pepper to taste.

5 Grill over direct medium-high heat 12 minutes on each side for medium-rare, 14 to 15 minutes per side for medium. (Cook 1-inch thick steaks 10 minutes for medium-rare or 12 minutes for medium.) Remove from the grill, place on a serving platter, and let rest for a few minutes. Carve the steak into serving pieces and top each with a coin of butter.

> **For the Butter:**
> 1 teaspoon olive oil
> 1 tablespoon minced garlic
> ¼ cup sun-dried tomatoes, minced
> 1 tablespoon fresh freshly squeezed lemon juice
> 1 tablespoon Worcestershire sauce
> 1 tablespoon minced fresh basil
> ½ cup Maytag blue cheese, crumbled
> ½ cup unsalted butter, cut into ½-inch slices
>
> **For the Porterhouse:**
> 1 porterhouse steak, 3½ to 4 pounds and 2 inches thick (or 4 steaks, about 16 ounces each and 1 inch thick)
> Salt and pepper

Pepper-Crusted Beef Tenderloin with Black Bean–Mango Salsa

The pink peppercorns used here are not true pepper, but the dried berries of a species of rose that grows in Madagascar. Like black and green "true" peppercorns, they bring out the full flavors of the rich steaks.

PREP TIME: 20 mins ★ GRILL TIME: 10 mins ★ SERVES 4

For the Salsa:

2 mangoes, peeled, pitted, and diced (about 1 cup)

1½ cups drained cooked (or canned) black beans

½ cup finely diced red bell pepper

¼ cup minced red onion

¼ cup minced fresh cilantro leaves

1 teaspoon dried red pepper flakes

Juice of 1 lime

Coarse salt

For the Tenderloin:

4 fillet mignon steaks, about 7 ounces each and 1½ inches thick

1 tablespoon Dijon mustard

½ tablespoon olive oil

3 tablespoons black peppercorns

1 tablespoon pink peppercorns

1 tablespoon green peppercorns

½ tablespoon coarse salt

1 Preheat and oil the grill. Bring the steaks to room temperature.

2 **For the Salsa,** combine all ingredients except salt in a small bowl and toss to mix. Season with salt to taste. Set aside.

3 **For the Tenderloin,** combine the mustard and olive oil in a small bowl and brush the steaks with the mixture. Using a mortar and pestle or peppermill, coarsely crush the peppercorns. Combine the peppercorns and salt on a plate and roll the steaks in the mixture, pressing to coat each side well.

4 Grill the steaks over direct medium-high heat for about 5 minutes per side for medium-rare, 6 to 7 minutes for medium, or to the desired doneness. Transfer to serving plates and serve with the salsa.

Chef's Tip: How to Dice a Mango

Hold the mango with the stem end down on a cutting board. Cut the fruit in half, about ½ inch from the center, just around the large flat seed. Repeat on the other side. Use a paring knife to score the flesh of each half into squares (do not cut through the outer skin). Push each half from the skin side so the squares pop out (it will look like a porcupine). Slice off the squares.

Filet Mignon with Compound Butter

The melting butter adds a little extra richness that complements the lean cut of meat.

PREP TIME: 15 mins ★ GRILL TIME: 10 mins ★ SERVES 4

1 For the Compound Butter, combine the butter, shallot, parsley, and lemon juice in the bowl of a food processor fitted with the metal blade. Process to blend. Transfer mixture to a sheet of plastic wrap. Roll into a log about 1½ inch thick and twist the ends to close. Refrigerate at least 1 hour or until firm. Remove from the refrigerator and slice into ½-inch coins when the steaks go on the grill.

2 Preheat and oil the grill. Bring the steaks to room temperature.

3 For the Filet Mignon, rub the steaks on all sides with oil and season with salt and pepper to taste. Grill over direct medium-high heat for about 5 minutes per side for medium-rare, 6 to 7 minutes per side for medium, or to the desired doneness.

4 Remove steaks from the grill and let rest for a few minutes. Place a slice of Compound Butter on top of each steak, allowing it to melt slightly before serving.

For the Compound Butter:
½ cup unsalted butter, at room temperature
1 shallot, minced
1 tablespoon minced fresh flat-leaf parsley
1 teaspoon freshly squeezed lemon juice
Salt and pepper

For the Filet Mignon:
4 filet mignon steaks, about 8 ounces each and 1½ inches thick
2 tablespoons canola oil
Salt and pepper

Filet Mignon with Caper Sauce

We like to serve this dish with Grilled Red Onions (page 146) and Coal-Baked Potatoes (page 146); the Caper Sauce is a natural flavor match for the sweet onions and fluffy potatoes. For an extra-special touch, garnish the dish with fried capers (see below).

PREP TIME: 20 mins ★ GRILL TIME: 10 mins ★ SERVES 4

For the Caper Sauce:
2 teaspoons canola oil
2 shallots, peeled and minced
2 cups beef broth
½ cup red wine
2 tablespoons balsamic vinegar
1 tablespoon capers, drained
Salt and pepper
1 tablespoon chopped fresh
    flat-leaf parsley

For the Steaks:
4 filet mignon steaks, about
    8 ounces each and 1½ inches
    thick
2 tablespoons canola oil
Salt and pepper

1 Preheat and oil the grill.

2 **For the Caper Sauce,** heat the oil in a small sauté pan over medium heat. Add the shallots and sauté for 3 minutes. Pour in the broth and wine and bring to a boil. Continue to boil for about 10 minutes or until the liquid has reduced to ½ cup. Stir in the vinegar and capers and season with salt and pepper to taste. Cook for 1 minute longer or until warm. When ready to serve, stir in the parsley.

3 **For the Steaks,** bring the steaks to room temperature. Rub them on all sides with the oil and then season with salt and pepper to taste. Grill the steaks over direct medium-high heat for about 5 minutes per side for medium-rare, 6 to 7 minutes per side for medium, or to the desired doneness. Remove from the grill and let rest for a few minutes. Serve the steaks with the caper sauce spooned over.

Chef's Tip: Fried Capers

Drain 1 bottle of capers in a colander. Line a baking sheet with paper towels. Spread the capers in a single layer and let dry 30 minutes. Line a plate with paper towels. Heat ¼ cup vegetable oil in a skillet over medium-high heat until hot but not smoking. Add the capers and fry 2 to 3 minutes or until the capers have opened and are golden. Remove capers with a slotted spoon and place on the paper towel–lined plate. Transfer capers to a serving dish and season with pepper. Capers will remain crisp if left uncovered up to 2 hours. Use them to garnish the dish above, as well as fish dishes (such as the Tuna Steaks with Hollandaise Sauce on page 101) or salads.

Santa Fe Grilled Rib-Eyes and Corn

The taste of the Southwest comes alive in these smoky steaks! You can use either boneless or bone-in rib-eyes; just remember that bone-in steaks take a little longer to cook.

PREP TIME: 35 mins ★ GRILL TIME: 20 mins ★ SERVES 4

1 Preheat and oil the grill. Peel the corn, leaving the husks attached at the base; remove silk. Rewrap corn in husks and tie closed with kitchen string. Soak in cold water 30 minutes.

2 Stir together steak sauce, garlic, chili powder, and cumin in a small bowl. Reserve ¼ cup.

3 Drain corn. Grill, uncovered, over indirect medium heat 20 to 30 minutes, turning frequently.

4 After 10 minutes, add steaks and grill over direct medium-high heat 5 to 6 minutes per side for medium-rare. During the last 5 minutes on the grill, brush the steaks with glaze. Remove the steaks from the grill and let rest a few minutes.

5 Meanwhile, combine reserved ¼ cup glaze and butter in a microwave-safe measuring cup. Microwave on high 1½ to 2 minutes, stirring once. Carefully peel corn; brush with chili butter. Serve steaks and corn with remaining chili butter on the side.

> 4 ears sweet corn, in husks
> ½ cup prepared steak sauce
> 2 cloves garlic, peeled and minced
> 1½ teaspoon chili powder
> ½ teaspoon ground cumin
> 4 rib-eye steaks
> 3 tablespoons unsalted butter

Mustard-Glazed Top Sirloin

*One of the great things about good steak is that it can stand up to assertive flavors,
like those in this glaze.*

PREP TIME: 5 mins ★ GRILL TIME: 8 mins ★ SERVES 4

4 top sirloin or boneless strip
 steaks, about 8 ounces each
 and 1 inch thick
2 tablespoons soy sauce
2 tablespoons dry sherry
2 tablespoons Dijon mustard
Juice of 1 lime
½ teaspoon dried thyme
½ teaspoon garlic salt
½ teaspoon freshly ground
 black pepper

1 Preheat and oil the grill. Bring the steaks to room temperature.

2 Place the soy sauce, sherry, mustard, lime juice, thyme, garlic
salt, and pepper in a small bowl and whisk together.

3 Brush the steaks on both sides with the glaze. Grill over
direct medium-high heat 4 minutes. Turn the steaks over, brush
again with the glaze, and grill 4 minutes longer for medium-
rare, 5 to 6 minutes for medium, or to the desired doneness.
Remove from the grill and let rest a few minutes before serving.

Chipotle-Glazed Strip Steaks

*Chipotle chiles are smoked dried jalapeños that can be found in the Mexican section of food markets
or gourmet and specialty food stores. They are sold canned in a spicy tomato sauce called adobo.*

PREP TIME: 5 mins ★ GRILL TIME: 8 mins ★ SERVES 4

½ cup olive oil
½ cup canned chipotles
 in adobo
½ cup freshly squeezed
 lemon juice
1 tablespoon honey
1 teaspoon fresh thyme leaves
½ teaspoon garlic salt
4 boneless strip steaks,
 about 8 ounces each and
 ⅞ inch thick

1 Preheat and oil the grill. Combine the oil, chipotles, lemon
juice, honey, thyme, and garlic salt in a blender and puree until
smooth. Arrange the steaks in a large, shallow baking dish and
pour the puree over. Cover and let sit at room temperature for
30 minutes, turning the steaks once or twice.

2 Grill the steaks over direct medium-high heat 3 to 4 minutes
on each side for medium-rare, about 5 minutes on each side for
medium, or to the desired doneness. Remove from the grill and
let rest a few minutes before serving.

Mustard-Glazed Top Sirloin

Grilled Fajitas

Fajitas make great party food! Serve with Salsa Fresca (page 53) and your favorite garnishes.

PREP TIME: **10 mins** ★ GRILL TIME: **12 mins** ★ SERVES **4**

8 (7-inch) flour tortillas
2 large onions, halved and sliced
3 tablespoons peanut oil
Salt and pepper
1 flank steak, about 2½ pounds
Juice of 1 lime
1½ teaspoons pure red chile powder

1 Preheat and oil the grill. Bring the steak to room temperature. Wrap the tortillas in heavy-duty aluminum foil and set aside.

2 Place the onions in a medium bowl. Add 2 tablespoons of the oil and season with salt and pepper to taste. Toss to coat well. Place in the center of a piece of heavy-duty aluminum foil. Fold the foil over the onions, sealing the folds to enclose them completely.

3 Stir together the remaining 1 tablespoon oil, lime juice, and chile powder in a small bowl. Season with salt and pepper to taste. Brush steak with mixture, then place the steak over direct medium-high heat and the onion packet over medium indirect heat. Grill the steak 6 to 7 minutes per side for medium-rare, 8 to 9 minutes for medium.

4 Move the onion packet around occasionally so that all of the onions are softened; this should take about as long as it takes the steak to cook.

5 About 5 minutes before the steak is done, place the tortilla packet over indirect medium heat and warm through.

6 Remove the steak, onions, and tortillas from the grill. Place the steak on a cutting board and let rest for 3 minutes. Using a sharp knife, cut the steak on the bias into very thin slices. Transfer the slices to a serving platter and spoon the onions over the top. Serve the tortillas on the side.

Chef's Tip: Salsa Fresca

Combine 1 pound plum tomatoes, diced; 3 tablespoons finely diced red onion; 2 tablespoons minced fresh cilantro; 1 seeded and minced jalapeño; the juice of 1 lime; 1 teaspoon coarse salt; and ½ teaspoon sugar in a medium bowl. Toss to mix. Let stand at least 30 minutes before serving.

Grilled Spiced Flank Steak

Mixed peppercorns, available at most supermarkets, are somewhat milder than plain black peppercorns. The sliced steak is also terrific as a salad topper.

PREP TIME: 5 mins ★ GRILL TIME: 12 mins ★ SERVES 4

1 Preheat and oil the grill. Bring the steak to room temperature.

2 Combine the mixed peppercorns with the cayenne, paprika, garlic salt, and celery salt in a small bowl. Generously coat both sides of the steak with the pepper mix.

3 Grill the steak over direct medium-high heat for 6 to 7 minutes per side for medium-rare or 8 to 9 minutes per side for medium.

4 Remove the steak from the grill and place on a cutting board to rest for 3 minutes. Cut on the bias into thin slices and serve.

1 flank steak, about 3 pounds
2 tablespoons ground mixed peppercorns
½ teaspoon cayenne pepper, or to taste
½ teaspoon hot paprika
½ teaspoon garlic salt, or to taste
½ teaspoon celery salt, or to taste

Honey-Glazed Beef Brisket

The honey and pineapple are a little sweet, but the smoky grill flavor keeps the sweetness in check. We like to serve this brisket with soft rolls, potato salad, and barbecue sauce, just like the barbecue you'd get in Texas.

PREP TIME: **10 mins** ★ COOK TIME: **2 hours** ★ GRILL TIME: **12 mins** ★ SERVES **4 to 6**

1 Combine the honey, mustard, pineapple juice, lemon juice, garlic, and thyme in a medium bowl, whisking to blend well. Season with salt and pepper to taste.

2 Place the brisket in a resealable plastic bag. Add the honey mixture, seal, and refrigerate at least 1 hour or up to 24 hours.

3 When ready to cook, preheat the oven to 350°F.

4 Transfer the brisket from the plastic bag to a nonstick roasting pan, discarding the plastic bag. Cover the pan with aluminum foil. Bake about 2 hours or until the brisket is very tender. About 15 minutes (or about 30 minutes if using a charcoal grill) before the brisket is ready, preheat and oil the grill.

5 Remove the brisket from the oven and transfer to the preheated grill. Grill, turning frequently, for about 12 minutes or until nicely charred. Remove from the grill and let rest a few minutes before slicing. Slice thinly against the grain and serve with sauce on the side.

---

1 cup orange blossom honey

½ cup grainy Dijon mustard

3 tablespoons pineapple juice

1 teaspoon freshly squeezed lemon juice

1 teaspoon minced garlic

1 teaspoon fresh thyme leaves

Salt and pepper

1 beef brisket, about 5 pounds, trimmed of excess fat

2 cups Original Barbecue Sauce, for serving (page 28)

London Broil with Grilled Mushrooms

This recipe can be made with almost any steak, except filet mignon. It also makes a terrific salad mixed with tomatoes and peppery greens such as arugula or watercress.

PREP TIME: 10 mins ★ GRILL TIME: 20 mins ★ SERVES 4

1 top round steak, about 2 pounds and 1½ inches thick

½ cup olive oil

½ cup balsamic vinegar

1 teaspoon freshly grated orange zest

4 tablespoons chopped fresh flat-leaf parsley

Salt and pepper

4 large portobello mushroom caps

1 Place the steak in a large resealable plastic bag along with the oil, vinegar, orange zest, and 1 tablespoon of the parsley. Seal the bag and push the steak around to coat well. Refrigerate 1 hour.

2 Preheat and oil the grill. Remove the steak and marinade from the refrigerator and bring to room temperature. Remove the steak from the bag and season with salt and pepper to taste.

3 Place the mushroom caps in the plastic bag. Seal the bag and push the mushrooms around to coat with marinade. Remove them from the bag and season with salt and pepper to taste. Discard the plastic bag.

4 Grill the steak over direct medium-high heat about 10 minutes on each side for medium-rare or 12 minutes on each side for medium. Grill the mushrooms at the same time, top side down, on the edge of the direct heat. Flip the mushrooms when you flip the steak and grill about 8 minutes longer, or until just beginning to char. Remove from the grill.

5 Remove the steak from the grill and let rest 5 minutes. Slice the steak and mushrooms into strips and arrange on a platter. Sprinkle with the remaining parsley and serve.

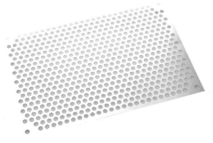

Chef's Tip: Grilled Wild Mushrooms

Grilling brings out the earthy goodness of wild mushrooms. Enoki, porcini, morel, shiitake, and oyster mushrooms are all delicious grilled. We suggest using a vegetable basket (page 15) or perforated grill pan (left). Just clean the mushrooms with a damp paper towel (mushrooms should not be rinsed; they will absorb water and will steam on the grill rather than caramelize). Toss mushrooms with a little olive oil, salt, and pepper, and spread into a single layer on the perforated pan or in the vegetable basket.

Orange-Flavored Beef Ribs

Grilled Radicchio (page 148) is a simple side that pairs well with these sweet and spicy ribs.

PREP TIME: 5 mins ★ COOK TIME: 1 hour ★ GRILL TIME: 5 mins ★ SERVES 4

1 Combine the vinegar, orange juice, molasses, soy sauce, brown sugar, paprika, and orange zest with hot pepper sauce to taste in a large resealable plastic bag. Add the ribs, seal, and knead the bag to coat the ribs. Refrigerate at least 1 hour or up to 24 hours.

2 When ready to cook, preheat the oven to 350°F.

3 Transfer the ribs, along with the marinade, from the plastic bag to a nonstick baking dish, discarding the plastic bag. Cover the entire dish with aluminum foil and place in the preheated oven. Bake 1 hour. About 15 minutes (or about 30 minutes if using a charcoal grill) before the ribs are ready, preheat and oil the grill.

4 Remove the ribs from the oven and transfer to the hot grill. Grill over direct medium heat about 5 minutes, turning frequently to prevent burning, or until nicely charred on all sides. Remove from the grill and serve.

> 1/2 cup white wine vinegar
> 1/2 cup freshly squeezed orange juice
> 1/2 cup molasses
> 1/2 cup soy sauce
> 2 tablespoons dark brown sugar
> 1 tablespoon sweet paprika
> 1 teaspoon freshly grated orange zest
> Hot pepper sauce
> 4 pounds beef ribs, trimmed of excess fat

Traditional Chophouse Mixed Grill

The mixed grill has been a chophouse favorite for generations.
It is usually served with a bowl of grainy mustard and some sour pickles.

PREP TIME: 10 mins ★ GRILL TIME: 20 mins ★ SERVES 4

1 sirloin steak, about 2 pounds

4 rib lamb chops

2 red onions, peeled and cut in half crosswise

1 cup peanut oil

Salt and pepper

2 tomatoes, cored and cut in half crosswise

½ cup dry unseasoned breadcrumbs

4 large button mushroom caps

2 slices calves' liver (about 1 pound)

4 thick slices slab bacon

1 Preheat and oil the grill. Bring the steak and lamb chops to room temperature.

2 Run a metal skewer through each onion half. Brush the cut sides of the onion halves with oil and season with salt and pepper to taste. Brush the cut side of each tomato half with oil, season with salt and pepper to taste, and sprinkle with breadcrumbs. Brush the mushrooms with oil and season with salt and pepper to taste. Set vegetables aside.

3 Rub the steak, liver, and lamb chops with oil and season with salt and pepper to taste.

4 Grill the steak over direct medium-high heat in the center of the grill for 10 minutes. Flip, then place the lamb next to the steak, with the liver, bacon, tomatoes, onions, and mushrooms surrounding the meat. Grill for 10 minutes longer or until the steak is medium-rare and the lamb medium, or to the desired doneness. After 6 minutes, begin checking the liver, bacon, and vegetables for doneness; do not overcook.

5 Remove the vegetables from the grill. Remove all of the meats from the grill and let rest. Remove the skewer from each onion. Cut the steak into slices and arrange an even amount on each serving plate. Place a lamb chop, a slice of liver, and a piece of bacon along with an onion half, a tomato half, and a mushroom on each plate.

"Ranchero" Beef Salad

Serve this hearty salad with Cowboy Cornbread (page 152) or Polenta Sticks (page 153).

PREP TIME: 25 mins ★ GRILL TIME: 8 mins ★ SERVES 4

1 Preheat and oil the grill. Bring the steaks to room temperature.

2 For the Dressing, mix all ingredients except the oils in a small bowl until blended. Slowly add the oils while whisking to blend. Season with salt and pepper to taste and set aside.

3 For the Steak, press the spice rub evenly on the steaks. Grill over direct medium-high heat 3 to 4 minutes on each side for medium-rare. Remove the steak from the grill, let it rest 5 minutes, and slice across the grain into ¼-inch-thick slices.

4 For the Salad, whisk the dressing to recombine. Place the lettuce in a large bowl, add about one-fourth of the dressing. Toss until the lettuce is coated. Pile on a serving platter. Arrange the steak over the center of the lettuce. Arrange the poblano, onion, tomatoes, and avocado around the steak. Sprinkle the radishes, cheese, and olives over the salad. Serve the remaining dressing on the side.

For the Lime-Chipotle Dressing:

1 canned chipotle chile, minced, plus 1 tablespoon adobo sauce, or to taste

2 garlic cloves, minced

3 tablespoons freshly squeezed lime juice

2 tablespoons white wine vinegar

¼ cup extra-virgin olive oil

¼ cup vegetable oil

Salt and pepper

For the Steak and Salad:

3 strip sirloin steaks, about 10 ounces each and 1 inch thick

4 tablespoons Savory Spice Rub (see page 23)

1 head romaine lettuce, torn into pieces

1 poblano chile, roasted, peeled, seeded, and sliced

½ red onion, sliced

12 cherry tomatoes

1 ripe avocado, peeled, pitted, and cut into large cubes

2 radishes, sliced

4 ounces blue cheese, crumbled

¼ cup pitted black olives, sliced

Beefstro Salad

This meaty take on the classic Cobb salad will be a surefire family favorite.
You can also use sirloin or flank steak in this salad; just be sure to adjust the grilling time.

PREP TIME: 10 mins ★ GRILL TIME: 10 mins ★ SERVES 4

For the Steaks:

1/3 cup oil from sun-dried tomatoes

2 tablespoons prepared blue cheese dressing

3 chuck eye steaks

For the Dressing and Salad:

1/3 cup drained oil-packed sun-dried tomatoes with herbs

3/4 cup blue cheese dressing

1/4 teaspoon freshly ground black pepper

1 package (10 ounces) mixed salad greens (about 8 cups)

2 medium avocados, diced

3/4 cup halved grape tomatoes

4 slices cooked bacon, crumbled

2 hard-boiled eggs, coarsely chopped

1 For the Steaks, combine sun-dried tomato oil and 2 tablespoons blue cheese dressing in a large resealable plastic bag. Add steaks and turn to coat. Close bag securely and marinate in refrigerator at least 15 minutes and up to 2 hours.

2 Meanwhile, for the Dressing, place sun-dried tomatoes in a food processor fitted with the metal blade. Cover; process until minced. Combine sun-dried tomatoes, remaining blue cheese dressing, and pepper in small bowl. Refrigerate, covered, until ready to serve.

3 Preheat and oil the grill. Remove steaks from marinade; discard marinade. Grill steaks over direct medium-high heat 5 to 6 minutes on each side for medium-rare. Remove the steak from the grill, let it rest 5 minutes, and slice across the grain into 1/4-inch-thick slices.

4 Arrange salad greens on large serving platter. Arrange steak slices, avocados, grape tomatoes, crumbled bacon, and eggs in rows over greens. Serve with dressing on the side.

Chef's Tip: Salad Switches

You can make this salad with any kind of lettuce you like. Chopped hearts of romaine would add a crisp texture and a pleasing bitter flavor; arugula has a peppery kick that pairs well with the blue cheese in the dressing. Add more vegetables, too, if you like. Fresh corn, chopped celery, or blanched asparagus, string beans, or sugar snap peas would all be great choices to add texture and flavor.

Beef Tenderloin Sandwich with Avocado and Black Beans

California avocados meet Miami-style black beans in this tasty sandwich.
Grill the rolls for even more smoky flavor.

PREP TIME: **10 mins** ★ GRILL TIME: **4 mins** ★ SERVES **4**

1 Preheat and oil the grill. Bring the steaks to room temperature.

2 Mash the avocado in a small bowl and season with salt and pepper to taste. Cover and set aside.

3 Mash the beans in a separate small bowl until mostly smooth. Season with salt and pepper to taste. Cover and set aside.

4 Lightly pound the steak slices to ⅛ inch thick. Season with salt and pepper and grill over direct medium-high heat for about 2 minutes on each side for medium.

5 Spread garlic, then beans on the bottom half of each roll and the mashed avocado on the top halves. Arrange 3 steak slices on top of the beans for each sandwich. Top with salsa, close the sandwiches, cut in half, and serve.

> 3 filet mignon steaks, about 5 ounces each and 1 inch thick, each cut horizontally into 4 slices
>
> 1 ripe avocado
>
> Coarse salt and freshly ground black pepper
>
> 1 cup black beans, drained
>
> 4 ciabatta rolls, split
>
> 2 tablespoons mashed roasted garlic (page 44)
>
> ¾ cup Salsa Fresca (page 53)

New York Strip BLT Sandwich

Cool the heat a little by using regular ketchup and Monterey Jack cheese.
You can also use havarti or Gouda in place of the pepper Jack, if you like.

PREP TIME: 8 mins ★ COOK TIME: 3 mins ★ GRILL TIME: 8 mins ★ MAKES 4 sandwiches

4 strip steaks, about 6 ounces and 1 inch thick

4 ciabatta buns, split in half

3/4 cup whole-grain mustard

3/4 cup prepared chipotle ketchup

8 slices pepper Jack cheese

8 slices peppered bacon, cooked

4 leaves romaine lettuce

2 beefsteak tomatoes, sliced

1 Preheat and oil the grill. Preheat the oven to 450°F. Bring the steaks to room temperature.

2 Grill the steaks over medium-high heat 3 to 4 minutes on each side for medium-rare. Remove the meat, let it rest for 5 minutes, and slice across the grain into ¼-inch thick slices.

3 Meanwhile, toast the buns on the edge of the grill 3 to 4 minutes, or until lightly marked and golden.

4 Spread the inner top of each bun with mustard and the bottom with chipotle ketchup.

5 Place the sliced steak on the bottom of each bun. Top each with 2 slices of pepper Jack cheese and 2 slices of bacon.

6 Place the sandwiches on a baking sheet and bake 3 to 4 minutes or until the cheese starts to melt. Top with the lettuce and tomatoes. Serve hot.

Chef's Tip: What's in a Name?

Strip steaks are cut from the strip loin and are sometimes sold under that name. They are also called club steaks, New York strips, shell steaks, or Delmonicos. So if you don't see "strip steaks" right away, look for one of the other names under which this tasty steak can be found.

New York–Style Hot Dogs

This classic New York-style sauce takes hot dogs from the everyday to the sublime. For the total experience, add brown mustard and sauerkraut along with the onion relish.

PREP TIME: 10 mins ★ COOK TIME: 25 mins ★ GRILL TIME: 6 mins ★ SERVES 6

1 Heat the oil in a heavy saucepan over medium heat. Add the onions and garlic along with 1 teaspoon salt. Cook, stirring frequently, about 5 minutes or until the onions are soft but have not taken on any color. Stir in the flour. When well-blended, add the tomato sauce, vinegar, brown sugar, cloves, and cayenne to taste along with 1 cup of water. Bring to a simmer and simmer about 15 minutes or until slightly thick. Remove from the heat. Taste and, if necessary, season with salt.

2 Preheat and oil the grill. Brush the cut sides of the buns with butter.

3 Place the hot dogs on the hot part of the grill and the buns around the edge. Grill the dogs for as long as you like—3 or 4 minutes for a little color up to 10 to 12 minutes for lots. Grill the buns just until nicely marked, about 1 minute.

4 Remove the buns and dogs from the grill. Place a dog in each bun and top with about ½ cup of the onion mixture.

2 tablespoons vegetable oil
4 cups chopped sweet onions
1 tablespoon minced garlic
1 teaspoon coarse salt, or more to taste
1 tablespoon all-purpose flour
1 cup tomato sauce
3 tablespoons white vinegar
2 tablespoons light brown sugar
Pinch ground cloves
Cayenne pepper
12 all-beef hot dogs
½ cup butter, melted
12 hot dog buns

Citrus-Sage Veal Chops

A classic side for veal is spaetzle, a traditional German dish. You can find dried spaetzle in your market's pasta aisle. Cook per the package directions, then toss with a little butter and chopped parsley.

PREP TIME: **5 mins** ★ GRILL TIME: **20 mins** ★ SERVES **4**

½ cup freshly squeezed lemon juice

2 tablespoons triple sec or other orange-flavored liqueur

1 tablespoon freshly squeezed lime juice

⅔ cup fresh orange juice

1 tablespoon freshly grated orange zest

1 tablespoon Dijon mustard

3 tablespoons chopped fresh sage

4 veal rib chops, about 12 ounces each and 1½ inches thick

Salt and pepper

---

1 Combine the lemon juice, triple sec, lime juice, orange juice and zest, mustard, and sage in a large resealable plastic bag. Add the chops and turn to coat. Seal and refrigerate 1 hour.

2 Preheat and oil the grill. Remove the chops from the marinade (discard marinade) and season with salt and pepper to taste. Grill over direct medium-high heat about 10 minutes on each side for medium-rare, about 12 minutes on each side for medium, or to the desired doneness. Remove from the grill and let rest 5 minutes before serving.

Veal Chops with Sweet and Sour Onions

Veal chops are so juicy and delicious they make any meal a special occasion. The sweet and smoky onions add depth and flavor to the dish.

PREP TIME: **10 mins** ★ COOK TIME: **25 mins** ★ GRILL TIME: **20 mins** ★ SERVES **4**

1 Preheat the oven to 350°F. Preheat and oil the grill.

2 Combine the onions with 2 tablespoons of the olive oil, the vinegar, wine, and brown sugar on a small nonstick baking sheet. Cover tightly with aluminum foil and bake 25 minutes or until very tender.

3 While the onions are baking, place the raisins in a small heatproof bowl. Add boiling water to cover and let stand 15 minutes or until plumped. Drain well and set aside.

4 Remove the onions from the oven and transfer to a medium bowl. Stir in the raisins and season with salt and pepper.

5 Combine the remaining ½ cup of olive oil with the rosemary and generously coat both sides of the chops with the oil mixture. Season with salt and pepper to taste. Grill over direct medium-high heat about 10 minutes on each side for medium-rare, about 12 minutes on each side for medium, or to the desired doneness. Remove the chops from the grill and let rest a few minutes. Serve each chop topped with a spoonful of onions; serve remaining onions on the side.

---

2 pounds (about 4 medium) red onions, cut into slivers

½ cup plus 2 tablespoons olive oil

2 tablespoons balsamic vinegar

2 tablespoons dry red wine

1 tablespoon light brown sugar

½ cup golden raisins

Salt and pepper

1 tablespoon chopped fresh rosemary

4 veal rib chops, about 12 ounces each and 1½ inches thick

Chef's Tip: No More Tears!

One challenge when using onions is how to keep your eyes from welling up with tears while cutting them. There are countless tricks that claim to help stop crying (placing a piece of onion on top of your head, covering your nose and mouth with a towel, holding a piece of bread in your mouth, not cutting through the root end, to name a few). There are even special "onion goggles" available for sale online. We've found that putting the whole peeled onion in the freezer for about 10 minutes before cutting it makes the onion release fewer fumes (and you release fewer tears).

Pork Tenderloin with Sesame Marinade

Toasted sesame oil and hoisin sauce are available in the Asian sections of most supermarkets, Asian markets, specialty food stores, and online. Take-out fried rice and steamed broccoli would complete this easy and delicious meal.

PREP TIME: 10 mins ★ GRILL TIME: 18 mins ★ SERVES 4

½ cup toasted (dark) sesame oil

½ cup toasted sesame seeds

½ cup unseasoned rice wine vinegar

½ cup "lite" soy sauce

½ cup hoisin sauce

2 tablespoons light brown sugar

2 teaspoons grated fresh ginger

1 teaspoon minced garlic

2 pork tenderloins, 9 to 12 ounces each, trimmed of all fat and silverskin

Salt and pepper

Sliced green onions, for garnish

1 Combine the sesame oil, sesame seeds, vinegar, soy sauce, hoisin sauce, brown sugar, ginger, and garlic in a large resealable plastic bag. Add the pork tenderloins and turn to coat. Seal the bag and refrigerate at least 1 hour or up to 24 hours.

2 Preheat and oil the grill. Remove the tenderloins from the plastic bag and bring to room temperature. Season with salt and pepper to taste. Grill over direct medium-high heat, turning occasionally, 18 to 20 minutes or until the internal temperature reaches 160°F.

3 Remove from the grill and set aside 5 minutes before slicing. Cut on the slight bias into thin slices, sprinkle with sliced green onions, and serve.

Chef's Tip: Pork Safety

At one time, well-done was the only way to eat pork. These days, with the more rigorous food-safety practices used in meat-processing plants and supermarket butchers, it is safe to consume pork cooked to medium (160°F) or medium-well (165°F). You can check the temperatures without losing tasty juices with an instant-read thermometer (page 15). The days of dry, tough pork chops and roasts are over!

Apple-Spice Marinated Pork Loin

Pork loin is denser than tenderloin and takes longer to cook on the grill. Watch carefully so it doesn't overcook, which will make it dry. We like it with Spicy Homemade Applesauce (page 154).

PREP TIME: **5 mins** ★ GRILL TIME: **1 hour 30 mins** ★ SERVES **4**

---

2 cups apple cider

1/2 cup dark brown sugar

2 tablespoons pure maple syrup

2 teaspoons prepared horseradish, well drained

1 teaspoon ground cinnamon

1/2 teaspoon ground cloves

1/2 teaspoon ground ginger

1/2 teaspoon cayenne pepper, or more to taste

3 pounds boneless pork loin, trimmed of excess fat

Salt and pepper

---

1 Whisk together the apple cider, brown sugar, maple syrup, horseradish, cinnamon, cloves, ginger, and cayenne in a medium bowl until blended.

2 Place the pork loin in a glass baking dish. Pour the marinade over the pork, turning to coat well. Cover and refrigerate 12 to 24 hours.

3 Preheat and oil the grill. Remove the pork from the marinade, letting any excess drain off. Reserve the marinade. Bring the pork to room temperature and season with salt and pepper to taste.

4 Grill the pork over direct medium heat, turning occasionally and brushing with the marinade, about 30 minutes. Move the loin to indirect heat, cover, and grill 1 hour or until the internal temperature reaches 160°F. Remove from the grill and let rest 5 minutes. Cut crosswise into 1/2-inch-thick slices and serve.

Grilled Glazed Pork Medallions

This sweet and spicy dish makes an elegant dinner party entrée. Brining the pork makes it even juicier. You can also make it with pork tenderloin or chicken or turkey cutlets.

PREP TIME: **10 mins** ★ GRILL TIME: **10 mins** ★ SERVES **4**

1 Combine 2 tablespoons salt, the granulated sugar and 4 cups cold water in a large resealable plastic bag. Add the pork loin, seal the bag, and let stand for 30 minutes.

2 While the pork is brining, prepare the glaze. Combine the jelly, vinegar, brown sugar, mustard, and hot pepper sauce to taste in a blender. Puree until smooth and transfer to a small bowl. Set aside.

3 Preheat and oil the grill. Remove the pork from the brine and pat dry. Cut it crosswise into 8 slices. Place each slice between 2 pieces of waxed paper and, using a kitchen mallet or small cast-iron frying pan, pound to flatten slightly.

4 Using a pastry brush, lightly coat both sides of the pork with the glaze and season with salt and pepper to taste. Grill the pork over direct medium-high heat, turning frequently, about 5 minutes on each side or until nicely glazed, golden, and cooked through, or until the internal temperature reaches 160°F. Remove from the grill and let rest 5 minutes.

2 tablespoons coarse salt, or more to taste
2 tablespoons granulated sugar
1 pound boneless pork loin
1 cup apple jelly
½ cup apple cider vinegar
2 tablespoons dark brown sugar
1 tablespoon Dijon mustard
Hot pepper sauce
Freshly ground black pepper

Chef's Tip: Brining Pork

Why brine? For one thing, it makes pork roasts and chops juicier and more flavorful when cooked using dry-heat methods such as roasting and grilling. It's also really easy and doesn't take much time. We recommend brining pork roasts and thick (1 inch or more) chops that are not being marinated prior to cooking. A simple brine recipe is 1 cup of coarse salt dissolved in 1 gallon of water, with flavorings such as sugar, herbs, and spices added to taste. Brining time depends on the size of the item being brined, but generally it is 30 minutes to 1 hour per pound.

Country-Style Barbecued Ribs

This recipe is a snap for summertime entertaining. Use a bottled barbecue sauce in place of the Moppin' Sauce if you're short on time.

PREP TIME: 5 mins ★ COOK TIME: 30 mins ★ GRILL TIME: 30 mins ★ SERVES 4

4 to 5 pounds country-style pork ribs

3 cups Moppin' Sauce (page 28)

1 Preheat the oven to 350°F. Bring the ribs to room temperature.

2 Place the ribs in a large baking pan. Add enough sauce to cover, stirring to coat well. Cover the pan with aluminum foil and roast 30 minutes or just until barely cooked.

3 Preheat and oil the grill. Remove the ribs from the oven and carefully scrape most of the sauce from them. Place the ribs on the grill, meat side down, over the hottest part of the grill. Grill, turning frequently, to sear and mark them, about 12 minutes. Transfer them to the edge of the grill and grill over medium heat, turning frequently, about 15 minutes or until cooked.

4 Remove from the grill and cut into individual ribs. Heat the remaining sauce and serve it on the side.

Chef's Tip: Pork Rib Primer

There are three kinds of pork ribs: country-style ribs, spareribs, and baby back ribs. Country-style are the meatiest of the three and usually only have five or six ribs to a rack. Spareribs are often found in Chinese cooking. They have a longer bone but less meat than baby backs. Baby back ribs are the most common type of pork ribs; they have more meat on them than spareribs but are less fatty than country-style ribs.

Spice-Rubbed Baby Back Ribs

Baby back ribs are a quintessential barbecue food. The combination of the spice rub and the barbecue sauce adds real flavor punch.

PREP TIME: 5 mins ★ GRILL TIME: 1 hour 30 mins ★ SERVES 4

1 Preheat and oil the grill. Brush the ribs with olive oil and coat with the rub on both sides, massaging it into the ribs with your fingers. Cover and let stand at room temperature for 30 minutes.

2 Place the ribs, meat side up, over indirect medium heat. Cover the grill, vent it slightly, and cook for about 1½ hours, turning occasionally. Brush the ribs with sauce a few times during the last 30 minutes of cooking. The ribs are done when no pink shows when they are pierced with a sharp knife. Meanwhile, heat the remaining sauce until warm. Cut the rack into individual ribs and serve with the sauce.

3 pounds baby back ribs, trimmed of fat and membrane

1 tablespoon olive oil

1 cup Savory Spice Rub (page 23)

3 cups Original Barbecue Sauce (page 28)

Kentucky Jack–Glazed Pork Chops

Fragrant with peaches and Kentucky sour mash, these are very special pork chops.
We like to serve them with grits, southern-style.

PREP TIME: 10 mins ★ GRILL TIME: 30 mins ★ SERVES 4

½ cup peach preserves

½ cup Kentucky sour mash or other fine quality bourbon

2 tablespoons peach liqueur

2 tablespoons freshly squeezed lemon juice

1 tablespoon freshly squeezed orange juice

½ cup grated onion

½ teaspoon ground nutmeg

½ teaspoon ground cinnamon

4 center-cut pork loin chops, about 8 ounces each and 1 inch thick, trimmed of excess fat

Salt and pepper

1 Combine preserves, bourbon, peach liqueur, lemon juice, and orange juice in a blender. Process until smooth and then add the onion, nutmeg, and cinnamon; blend again to incorporate.

2 Place the pork chops in a shallow nonreactive baking dish. Pour the marinade over the chops, turning to coat all sides. Cover the entire dish with aluminum foil and refrigerate at least 1 hour or up to 24 hours.

3 Preheat and oil the grill. Remove the chops from the marinade, letting any excess drain off, and bring to room temperature. Season with salt and pepper to taste; reserve the marinade.

4 Grill the pork chops over direct medium-high heat, turning occasionally and brushing with the marinade, about 15 minutes. Continue grilling another without basting 15 minutes or until the internal temperature reaches 160°F. Remove from the grill and let rest 5 minutes before serving.

Jerked Pork Chops

Jerk is the name given to the fiery Jamaican seasoning mix typically used for chicken. If you cannot find habanero chiles (which are among the hottest chiles in the world), substitute 2 tablespoons hot chile sauce. We like to serve these fiery chops with Jet-Fresh Pineapple Sauce (page 27) or Black Bean–Mango Salsa (page 46).

PREP TIME: **10 mins** ★ GRILL TIME: **14 mins** ★ SERVES **4**

1 Combine all ingredients except the pork chops in the bowl of a food processor and puree until smooth. Place the pork chops in a large glass baking dish and cover with the jerk paste. Cover and refrigerate for 2 to 3 hours, turning occasionally.

2 Preheat and oil the grill. Remove the pork chops from the refrigerator and bring to room temperature. Leave as much of the paste on the chops as possible and grill over direct medium heat about 7 minutes per side for medium, 8 minutes for medium-well, or until the internal temperature reaches 160°F. Remove from the grill and let rest 5 minutes before serving.

1 red onion, chopped

3 fresh habanero or Scotch bonnet chiles, seeded and chopped

1/2 cup freshly squeezed lime juice

3 tablespoons ground allspice

2 tablespoons minced fresh ginger

2 tablespoons soy sauce

2 tablespoons olive oil

1 tablespoon honey

1 tablespoon chopped garlic

1/2 tablespoon minced fresh thyme leaves

1/2 tablespoon salt

1 teaspoon ground cinnamon

1 teaspoon freshly ground black pepper

1/2 teaspoon ground nutmeg

4 pork rib chops, about 12 ounces each and 1 inch thick

✎ Chef's Tip: Hot Pepper Safety

Hot peppers such as habaneros and Thai bird chiles are deliciously spicy, but should be handled with care. We recommend wearing rubber gloves when when working with them. Even with gloves, be sure to wash your hands throughly after touching these fiery ingredients.

Butterflied Leg of Lamb with Eggplant Compote

"Butterflying" the leg of lamb refers to the technique of cutting the lamb not quite completely through and opening the halves like a book. Have your butcher butterfly the lamb for you.

PREP TIME: 10 mins ★ GRILL TIME: 45 mins ★ SERVES 4 to 6

1 **For the Lamb,** combine the ½ cup olive oil with the lemon juice, celery seed, and cumin. Generously coat the lamb with the oil mixture, reserving remaining oil. Let lamb stand at room temperature 30 minutes. Preheat and oil the grill.

2 **For the Compote,** generously coat the eggplant and tomatoes with olive oil. Season with salt and pepper. Grill the eggplant over direct medium heat, turning occasionally, about 8 minutes or until charred and just cooked through. Grill the tomatoes, stem end down, without turning, about 4 minutes or until slightly soft. Remove the vegetables from the grill. Peel the skin from the tomatoes and discard. Cut each tomato in half.

3 Combine the eggplant, tomatoes, onion, olives, and garlic in the bowl of a food processor fitted with a metal blade. Pulse until just chopped. Transfer to a medium bowl and stir in the vinegar, sugar, and capers. Season with salt and pepper to taste and let stand at room temperature while grilling the lamb.

4 Season the lamb with salt and pepper to taste. Grill over direct medium heat 12 minutes, turning and occasionally brushing with the oil mixture. Move the lamb over indirect heat, cover, and grill, turning and occasionally brushing with oil, 18 to 20 minutes longer for medium-rare (internal temperature is 150°F) or about 25 minutes longer for medium (internal temperature is 160°F).

5 Remove the lamb from the grill and let rest 10 minutes before slicing. Stir the parsley into the compote and serve with the lamb.

For the Lamb:

½ cup extra-virgin olive oil

1 tablespoon freshly squeezed lemon juice

1 tablespoon celery seed

1 teaspoon ground cumin

3½ pounds boneless leg of lamb

For the Compote:

1 large eggplant, about 1 pound, trimmed and cut crosswise into ½-inch thick slices

4 large tomatoes, cored

½ cup extra-virgin olive oil

Salt and pepper

1 small sweet onion, chopped

½ cup chopped pitted green olives

1 tablespoon roasted garlic (page 44)

1 tablespoon red wine vinegar

2 teaspoons sugar

2 teaspoons chopped drained capers

1 tablespoon chopped fresh flat-leaf parsley

Leg of Lamb with Tomato-Ginger Sauce

Leg of lamb is usually butterflied for grilling,
but a small one can be grilled whole, as in this recipe.

PREP TIME: 10 mins ★ COOK TIME: 5 mins ★ GRILL TIME: 45 mins ★ SERVES 4

For the Lamb:

1 small leg of lamb, about 3½ pounds, trimmed of excess fat

¼ cup olive oil

Salt and pepper

For the Sauce:

1 cup peeled, seeded, and chopped tomatoes

1 tablespoon grated fresh ginger

1 teaspoon minced garlic

¼ cup dry white wine

2 tablespoons olive oil

¼ cup chopped fresh mint

Salt and pepper

1 For the Lamb, generously coat the lamb with ¼ cup oil, season with salt and pepper to taste, and let stand at room temperature 30 minutes. Preheat and oil the grill.

2 Grill the lamb over direct medium-high heat, turning occasionally, about 15 minutes or until seared on all sides. Move to indirect heat on the coolest part of the grill and cover. Grill about 30 minutes, turning occasionally, for medium-rare, (or to an internal temperature of 150°F), 35 minutes for medium (internal temperature of 160°F), or to the desired doneness.

3 Meanwhile, for the Sauce, combine the tomatoes, ginger, and garlic in the bowl of a food processor fitted with a metal blade. Pulse to make a chunky mix. Transfer mixture to a small nonreactive saucepan and heat over medium heat. Add the wine along with the 2 tablespoons olive oil and season with salt and pepper to taste. Bring to a simmer and continue to simmer about 3 minutes. Remove from the heat and stir in the mint. Keep warm until ready to serve.

4 Remove the lamb from the grill and let rest 5 minutes. Slice and serve with the sauce on the side.

Chef's Tip: Grilled Garlic Bread

Cut a loaf of crusty Italian bread into ½-inch slices. Lightly brush both sides of each slice with olive oil. Grill cut side down on the edge of the grill until marked and golden, 2 to 4 minutes on each side. Cut 2 or 3 cloves of garlic across the widest part of the cloves. Remove the bread from the grill and rub each slice with the cut side of a clove of garlic. Serve warm.

Fennel-Dusted Lamb Chops with Garlic Glaze

Serve these chops with Grilled Asparagus and Spring Onions (page 146).
The earthy flavor of mushrooms is also a good partner for lamb.

PREP TIME: 5 mins ★ GRILL TIME: 8 mins ★ SERVES 4

1 Preheat and oil the grill. Bring the lamb chops to room temperature.

2 Combine the fennel, salt, pepper, and thyme in a shallow bowl. Press both sides of each chop into the mixture. Set aside.

3 Combine the oil and garlic in a small bowl and mash gently until blended. Lightly brush both sides of each chop with the garlic mixture and grill over direct medium-high heat about 4 minutes on each side for medium-rare, 5 minutes on each side for medium, or to the desired doneness. Brush with the remaining glaze while grilling. Remove the chops from the grill and let rest 5 minutes before serving.

8 bone-in lamb loin chops, about 5 ounces each and 1 inch thick

2 tablespoons ground fennel

1 tablespoon coarse salt

1/2 tablespoon freshly cracked black pepper

1/2 tablespoon ground dried thyme

1/2 cup olive oil

1/2 tablespoon roasted garlic (page 44)

Mint-Glazed Lamb Chops with Mint-Cucumber Sauce

Here's an update on lamb with mint jelly. Rosemary Grilled Potatoes (page 158) go well with the lamb (and are great dipped into the Mint-Cucumber Sauce).

PREP TIME: 10 mins ★ COOK TIME: 5 mins ★ GRILL TIME: 20 mins ★ SERVES 4

For the Mint-Glazed Lamb Chops:

8 thick rib or loin lamb chops, about 6 ounces each and 2 inches thick

$1/2$ cup freshly squeezed grapefruit juice

3 tablespoons light brown sugar

2 tablespoons mint jelly

$1/2$ cup minced fresh mint

Salt and pepper

For the Mint-Cucumber Sauce:

$1/2$ cup sour cream

2 tablespoons freshly squeezed orange juice

$1/2$ cup minced cucumber

$1/2$ cup minced fresh mint

1 tablespoon minced red onion

Salt and pepper

1 Preheat and oil the grill. Bring the lamb to room temperature.

2 For the Sauce, place the sour cream and orange juice in a small mixing bowl and stir vigorously to smooth. Add the cucumber, mint, and onion, stirring to combine. Season with salt and pepper to taste and set aside.

3 For the Lamb, combine the grapefruit juice, brown sugar, and jelly in a small saucepan over medium heat. Bring to a simmer, stirring constantly, and simmer 1 to 2 minutes or just until the sugar has dissolved. Remove from the heat and stir in the mint.

4 Brush both sides of the chops with glaze. Season with salt and pepper to taste. Grill, basting with glaze and turning occasionally, over direct medium-high heat 8 to 10 minutes on each side for medium or to the desired doneness. Remove from the grill and let rest 5 minutes before serving with the Mint-Cucumber Sauce.

Yogurt-Marinated Lamb Chops

A yogurt marinade is a simple and traditional way to tenderize meat. Don't leave the lamb in the marinade for more than 3 hours or it will become soggy instead of tenderized.

PREP TIME: 10 mins ★ GRILL TIME: 15 mins ★ SERVES 4

1 Combine the yogurt, garlic, ginger, cumin, coriander, cinnamon, turmeric, and cayenne in a large resealable plastic bag. Seal and squeeze to mix. Add the chops, seal the bag, and push the chops around to coat all sides. Refrigerate 30 minutes or up to 3 hours.

2 Preheat and oil the grill. Remove the chops from the marinade and scrape off any excess; discard the marinade. Bring the lamb to room temperature. Season the chops with salt and pepper to taste. Grill, turning occasionally, 7 or 8 minutes on each side for medium or to the desired doneness. Remove from the grill and let rest 5 minutes before serving.

1 cup nonfat yogurt
4 cloves garlic, minced
1 tablespoon grated ginger
1 teaspoon ground cumin
1 teaspoon ground coriander
1/2 teaspoon ground cinnamon
1/2 teaspoon ground turmeric
1/2 teaspoon cayenne pepper, or to taste
8 bone-in double lamb chops, about 6 ounces each and 1 1/2 inches thick, trimmed of excess fat
Salt and pepper

Chef's Tip: Marinating Lamb

If you want to experiment with different marinades for lamb, just keep in mind that the marinade needs to include some kind of acid to cut lamb's natural fattiness. This can be as simple as lemon juice or red wine vinegar. Just combine it in a 1-to-1 ratio of acid to other ingredients (meaning, if you use 1 cup of lemon juice, all of your other flavorings should combine to equal 1 cup also).

Pecan-Crusted Rack of Lamb

The crust works just as well with individual lamb chops or steaks if you prefer.
Serve with mashed potatoes and Wilted Mustard Greens (page 148).

PREP TIME: **10 mins** ★ COOK TIME: **12 mins** ★ GRILL TIME: **10 mins** ★ SERVES **4**

---

2 racks of lamb (8 ribs each),
    about 4 pounds total

Salt and pepper

1/2 cup pecan pieces, finely
    chopped

1/2 cup coarse fresh bread
    crumbs

1/2 cup honey

2 tablespoons Dijon mustard

1 tablespoon olive oil

1 teaspoon minced garlic

1/2 tablespoon fresh thyme
    leaves

---

1 Preheat and oil the grill. Preheat the oven to 325°F. Cut each lamb rack in half and bring to room temperature.

2 Season lamb with salt and pepper to taste. Grill, fat side down, over direct medium-high heat for 5 minutes on each side. Using tongs, hold the racks vertically over the grill to sear the ends. Remove from the grill and let rest 10 minutes.

3 Meanwhile, place the pecans and bread crumbs on a plate and combine. Place the honey, mustard, olive oil, garlic, and thyme in a large shallow bowl and whisk to combine.

4 Dip the lamb in the honey mixture, then into the crust mixture, pressing down to make sure the crust adheres to the meat. Use your fingers to pack the crust on the meat if necessary. Transfer to a roasting pan and finish in the oven 12 to 14 minutes for medium-rare, 15 to 17 minutes for medium, or to the desired doneness. Remove the lamb from the oven and let rest 10 minutes. Cut into chops and serve.

Southwest-Style Buffalo Steaks with Green Chile Sauce

If you can't find buffalo steaks, which are leaner with lower fat and cholesterol than beef, use beef rib-eyes. The green chile sauce is a mild sauce that can be used on any meat or poultry.

PREP TIME: 10 mins ★ COOK TIME: 45 mins ★ GRILL TIME: 22 mins ★ SERVES 4

For the Southwest-Style Buffalo Steaks:

4 boneless buffalo rib-eye steaks, about 12 ounces each and 1½ inches thick

2 tablespoons pure red chile powder

Salt and pepper

For the Green Chile Sauce:

1 pound fresh mild green chiles, such as Anaheim or Hatch (New Mexico)

2 tablespoons peanut oil

1 cup chopped sweet onions

1 teaspoon minced garlic

1 cup chicken broth

---

1 Preheat the oven to 450°F. Preheat and oil the grill.

2 **For the Steaks,** season both sides of the steaks with the chile powder. Season with salt and pepper to taste. Bring to room temperature.

3 **For the Sauce,** place the chiles on a nonstick baking pan and roast 20 minutes or until well charred. Remove from the oven and let stand until cool enough to handle. Peel off the charred skin and remove the stems and seeds. Roughly chop the chiles.

4 Heat the oil in a large saucepan over medium heat. Add the onions and garlic and sauté 3 minutes or until translucent. Add the chopped chiles and the broth. Season with salt and pepper to taste. Bring to a simmer and simmer 20 minutes or until very thick.

5 Remove the pan from the heat. Pour half the chile mixture into a blender. Holding down the top of the blender with a kitchen towel (to prevent the heat from pushing the top off), process until smooth. Pour into a bowl. Repeat with remaining chile mixture. Let stand at room temperature until serving.

6 Grill the steaks over direct medium-high heat 12 minutes on the first side. Turn the steaks and grill on the other side about 10 minutes for medium-rare, 12 to 14 minutes for medium, or to the desired doneness. Remove the steaks from the grill and let rest 5 minutes before serving with the sauce on the side.

Chef's Tip: About Buffalo

In the late 1800s, buffalo (aka bison) had been hunted nearly to extinction. After strict protective measures were put in place, the herds were able to thrive well enough to become a viable source of meat again.

Mustard-Marinated Rabbit

Rabbit is very similar in flavor to chicken, but the meat is much leaner.

PREP TIME: 10 mins ★ GRILL TIME: 15 mins ★ SERVES 4

1 Place the rabbit in a glass baking dish. Whisk together the mustard, oil, orange juice concentrate, onion, thyme, and rosemary in a small bowl until smooth. Season with salt and pepper to taste. Pour over the rabbit, tossing to coat well. Cover and refrigerate 1 hour.

2 Preheat and oil the grill.

3 Remove the rabbit from the marinade and scrape off any excess marinade. Reserve the marinade. Grill the rabbit over direct medium-high heat, turning occasionally and brushing with the reserved marinade, 10 minutes, or until marked. Cover and grill, turning occasionally, 5 minutes more or until cooked through. Serve hot.

> 1 rabbit, about 4 pounds, cut into 4 equal pieces
> ½ cup Dijon mustard
> ½ cup extra-virgin olive oil
> 2 tablespoons orange juice concentrate
> 2 tablespoons minced onion
> 1 teaspoon fresh thyme leaves
> 1 teaspoon chopped fresh rosemary needles
> Salt and pepper

BBQ Chicken with Cucumber Relish

Poultry

BBQ Chicken with Cucumber Relish ★ 86

Cilantro-Lime Chicken Strips ★ 86

Grilled Lemon Chicken ★ 87

Deviled Chicken Drummers ★ 88

Basil Chicken BLT ★ 90

BBQ Chicken Sandwich with Red Pepper Aioli ★ 91

Grilled Turkey with Cranberry Relish ★ 92

Duck Breasts with Orange-Cherry Sauce ★ 93

BBQ Chicken with Cucumber Relish

Add a few sliced tomatoes and some fresh corn and you have a perfect light summer meal!

PREP TIME: **15 mins** ★ GRILL TIME: **12 mins** ★ SERVES **4**

For the BBQ Chicken:

1 cup light unsweetened coconut milk

½ cup freshly squeezed lime juice

2 tablespoons vegetable oil

1 tablespoon minced garlic

1 tablespoon chopped fresh cilantro

1 tablespoon snipped fresh chives

1 teaspoon chopped jalapeño

8 boneless, skinless chicken breast halves

Salt and pepper

For the Cucumber Relish:

2 large cucumbers, chopped

½ cup chopped fresh mint

1 tablespoon minced garlic

1 teaspoon freshly grated lemon zest

½ cup rice wine vinegar

1 tablespoon sugar

1 For the Chicken, combine the coconut milk, lime juice, oil, garlic, cilantro, chives, and jalapeño in a large resealable plastic bag. Add the chicken, seal, and roll around to coat evenly. Refrigerate at least 1 hour or up to 12 hours.

2 Meanwhile, for the Relish, combine the ingredients in a small bowl and toss to mix. Let stand at room temperature until ready to serve.

3 Preheat and oil the grill. Remove the chicken from the marinade; discard marinade. Season chicken with salt and pepper to taste. Grill, turning frequently, about 6 minutes on each side or until just cooked through. Remove from the grill and serve with the relish on the side.

Cilantro-Lime Chicken Strips

You can thread the chicken strips on skewers before grilling; the grilling time is the same.

PREP TIME: **15 mins** ★ GRILL TIME: **6 mins** ★ SERVES **4**

½ cup olive oil

½ cup freshly squeezed lime juice

1½ cups fresh cilantro leaves

1 serrano chile, chopped

1 teaspoon sugar

1 teaspoon chopped garlic

Salt and pepper

8 boneless, skinless chicken breast halves

1 Cut each chicken breast lengthwise into 3 strips and set aside. Combine the oil, lime juice, cilantro, serrano, sugar, and garlic in a blender. Puree until smooth. Season with salt and pepper to taste. Reserve ½ cup of the marinade; transfer the rest to a glass baking dish. Add the chicken strips to the dish and toss to coat. Cover and refrigerate 2 hours.

2 Preheat and oil the grill. Remove the chicken from the marinade; discard marinade. Grill over direct medium-high heat 3 minutes per side or until cooked through. Brush with the reserved ½ cup of the marinade and serve.

Grilled Lemon Chicken

This grilled chicken is very succulent and juicy.
Serve with plenty of crusty bread to soak up the hot juices.

PREP TIME: **10 mins** ★ GRILL TIME: **30 mins** ★ SERVES **4**

Juice of 3 lemons

Feshly grated zest of 1 lemon

½ cup olive oil

1 tablespoon chopped fresh
  rosemary needles

2 chickens, about 3 pounds
  each, split in half

Salt and pepper

4 lemons, cut in half crosswise

Extra-virgin olive oil, for drizzling

1 Combine the lemon juice and zest with the olive oil and rosemary in a glass baking dish. Add the chickens and toss to coat. Cover and refrigerate at least 2 hours or up to 12 hours.

2 Preheat and oil the grill. Remove the chickens from the marinade, season with salt and pepper to taste, and transfer them to the grill. Grill over indirect medium-high heat, about 30 minutes or until an instant-read thermometer reads 180°F when inserted into the thickest part of the thigh.

3 About 5 minutes before the chickens are ready, place the lemon halves, cut side down, on the grill. Grill until very hot and juicy, about 5 minutes.

4 Remove the chickens from the grill, drizzle with extra-virgin olive oil, and serve with warm lemon halves on the side.

Deviled Chicken Drummers

A perforated pan placed on the grill grid keeps the coating from falling off during the final cooking. You can replace the cayenne with paprika if you prefer a less spicy version.

PREP TIME: 5 mins ★ GRILL TIME: 25 mins ★ SERVES 4

3 cups fresh bread crumbs

1 tablespoon chopped fresh parsley

Cayenne pepper

1/2 cup unsalted butter, melted

1/2 cup Dijon mustard

2 tablespoons Worcestershire sauce

Salt

8 to 10 skin-on chicken drumsticks

1 Preheat and oil the grill. Combine the bread crumbs, parsley, and cayenne to taste in a shallow baking dish. Set aside.

2 Combine the butter, mustard, and Worcestershire sauce in a small bowl. Season with salt to taste.

3 Brush the chicken legs with a generous amount of the butter mixture, coating well. Grill, over direct medium heat, turning and basting frequently with the butter, 20 minutes or until marked and nearly cooked through.

4 Remove the chicken legs from the grill and carefully roll them in the seasoned bread crumbs until coated, pressing the crumbs to help them adhere. (Rubber gloves will keep your hands from getting too hot as you coat the chicken.)

5 Grill 5 minutes longer or until an instant-read thermometer reads 160°F when inserted into the thickest part. Serve hot.

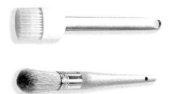

Chef's Tip: Basting Brushes

Basting foods on the grill is much easier with a silicone brush (top). Silicone doesn't melt when it comes in contact with heat (up to 500°F), so it is ideal for use on the grill. Standard basting brushes are also handy, but are better suited for lower-heat cooking like smoking or slow roasting.

Basil Chicken BLT

Make this classic sandwich special with rustic sourdough or multigrain bread.

PREP TIME: 20 mins ★ GRILL TIME: 12 mins ★ SERVES 4

4 boneless chicken breast
halves, skin-on, about 4
ounces each

½ cup olive oil, plus more for
brushing

2 tablespoons balsamic vinegar

2 tablespoons chopped fresh
basil, divided

Salt and pepper

8 (½-inch-thick) slices rustic
bread

½ cup mayonnaise

4 large leaves Boston lettuce

8 (½-inch-thick) slices tomato

12 slices cooked thick-cut bacon

1 Preheat and oil the grill. Place the chicken breasts in a glass baking dish. Stir together the olive oil, vinegar, and 1 tablespoon basil. Pour over the chicken and toss to coat well. Set aside 15 minutes.

2 Season the chicken with salt and pepper to taste. Grill, skin side down, over direct medium-high heat about 5 minutes on each side or until the chicken is cooked through. Remove chicken from the grill and set aside.

3 Lightly brush one side of each bread slice with olive oil. Grill, oiled side down, 1 minute or just until marked and golden. Turn and grill the other side 1 minute.

4 Stir together the mayonnaise and the remaining basil. Place 4 slices of the bread, oiled side up, on a work surface. Generously coat each piece with the basil mayonnaise.

5 Remove the skin from the chicken and cut each breast on the bias into thin slices, keeping each breast together. Lay 1 breast on each mayonnaise-covered bread slice. Top each with lettuce, 2 slices of tomato, and 3 strips of bacon.

6 Coat the oiled side of the remaining 4 slices of bread with the remaining mayonnaise. Top each sandwich, pressing down to compact slightly. Cut the sandwiches in half and serve.

BBQ Chicken Sandwich with Red Pepper Aioli

The grilled red pepper aioli adds a sweet and smoky flavor to this classic sandwich.

PREP TIME: **10 mins** ★ GRILL TIME: **20 mins** ★ SERVES **4**

1 Place the chicken breasts in a resealable plastic bag, seal. and gently pound them to a ½-inch thickness. Cut the breasts in half crosswise and transfer to another large plastic resealable bag. Add 2 cups of the Barbecue Sauce, seal, and refrigerate 2 hours.

2 Preheat and oil the grill. Remove the chicken from the sauce (discard sauce), cover, and let stand at room temperature 20 minutes. Heat the remaining ½ cup sauce in a small saucepan until warmed through. Grill the chicken over direct medium heat for 4 to 5 minutes per side, brushing with warm sauce 2 or 3 times. Remove from the grill and set aside.

3 Grill the bell pepper over direct medium heat for 8 to 10 minutes, turning occasionally, until charred and soft. Remove and let stand until cool enough to handle. Remove the charred skin and discard. Roughly chop the pepper and place in a blender. Add the mayonnaise, mustard, garlic, lemon juice, and salt, and pulse until smooth.

4 Spread one cut side of each roll with aioli. Top with chicken and the greens. Cover with tops of rolls and cut in half. Serve with the remaining Barbecue Sauce on the side.

8 boneless, skinless chicken breast halves, about 4 ounces each
2½ cups Original Barbecue Sauce (page 28)
4 ciabatta rolls, split lengthwise in half
4 cups mesclun greens
1 red bell pepper, cut in half and seeded
2 tablespoons mayonnaise
½ teaspoon Dijon mustard
½ teaspoon minced garlic
½ tablespoon freshly squeezed lemon juice
½ teaspoon salt

Grilled Turkey with Cranberry Relish

Thanksgiving on the grill? Why not? If you are using a charcoal grill, you will have to watch it carefully to keep a steady low heat, adding coals about every 30 to 45 minutes to maintain the grill temperature.

PREP TIME: 15 mins ★ COOK TIME: 30 mins ★ GRILL TIME: 3 hours ★ SERVES 4 to 6

For the Grilled Turkey:

One 10- to 12-pound turkey, rinsed and patted dry

1 lemon, cut in half

About ½ cup peanut oil

Coarse salt and black pepper

2 large apples, washed

2 large onions, peeled

For the Cranberry Relish:

1 pound cranberries

1 cup canned crushed pineapple

1 whole seedless orange, chopped

½ cup chopped candied ginger

½ cup raisins

½ cup chopped walnuts

½ teaspoon ground cinnamon

1 cup sugar, or to taste

1 Preheat and oil the grill. Place an oven thermometer in the grill. Place a pan of water under the grill rack or on the side.

2 For the Turkey, rub the turkey inside and out with the cut sides of the lemon, then rub with peanut oil. Season the turkey inside and out with salt and pepper to taste. Place the apples and onions in the cavity.

3 When the grill temperature reaches 350°F, place the turkey on the grill. Cover and grill over indirect heat about 3 hours, continually maintaining a temperature of at least 325°F and no more than 350°F.

4 Meanwhile, for the Relish, combine the cranberries, pineapple, orange, ginger, raisins, walnuts, and cinnamon in a medium heavy saucepan over medium heat. Add the sugar and stir until it dissolves. Simmer 15 minutes or until thick. Add more sugar if necessary and cook until the sugar has dissolved. Remove from the heat and set aside to cool.

5 When an instant-read thermometer inserted into the thickest part of the thigh reads 180°F, remove the turkey from the grill. Allow turkey to rest for 10 minutes before carving. Remove the apples and onions from the cavity, chop, and combine. Serve carved turkey with the apple-onion mixture and cranberry relish on the side.

Chef's Tip: Brining a Turkey

Brining a turkey requires a little planning, but it's not difficult and the results are worth it. Heat 1 cup coarse salt, ½ cup honey, 1 gallon chicken stock, 1 teaspoon cracked black pepper, 1 tablespoon juniper berries, and 1 cinnamon stick in a stock pot over medium heat, stirring until the salt is dissolved. Bring to a boil. Remove the pan from the heat and refrigerate 2 hours or until cold. At least 6 hours before cooking, place the turkey in a 5-gallon bucket. Combine the cold brine and 1 gallon ice water, pour over the turkey, and set a plate on top to keep the bird submerged. Refrigerate, flipping the turkey top to bottom halfway through the brining time. Just before cooking, remove the turkey from the brine, rinse inside and out, and pat dry.

Duck Breasts with Orange-Cherry Sauce

Grilled Polenta Sticks (page 153) go well with the sweet sauce and the duck's intense flavor.

PREP TIME: **25 mins** ★ COOK TIME: **5 mins** ★ GRILL TIME: **8 mins** ★ SERVES **4**

1 For the Duck, combine the olive oil with 2 tablespoons balsamic vinegar, mustard, honey, thyme, and sage in a large resealable plastic bag. Add the duck, seal, and knead the bag to cover the breasts with the marinade. Refrigerate at least 2 hours or up to 6 hours.

2 Meanwhile, for the Sauce, place the dried cherries in a heatproof bowl and cover with boiling water by at least 1 inch. Let stand 15 minutes or until plumped; drain.

3 Combine the marmalade, vinegars, and orange liqueur in a small saucepan over medium heat. Bring to a simmer and add the drained cherries. Cook about 5 minutes or until syrupy. Season with salt and pepper to taste. Remove the pan from the heat and set aside.

4 Preheat and oil the grill. Remove the duck from the marinade, scraping off excess; discard marinade. Season with salt and pepper to taste. Grill 4 minutes on each side for medium-rare.

5 Remove the breasts from the grill and let rest 3 minutes. Cut on the bias into thin slices, fan each one on a plate, and spoon the sauce over the top. Sprinkle with chives and serve.

For the Duck Breasts:
1/2 cup olive oil
2 tablespoons balsamic vinegar
1 tablespoon Dijon mustard
1 tablespoon honey
1 teaspoon minced fresh thyme
1 teaspoon minced fresh sage
4 boneless, skinless duck breast halves
Salt and pepper

For the Orange-Cherry Sauce:
1/2 cup dried cherries
1/2 cup orange marmalade
6 tablespoons balsamic vinegar
2 tablespoons champagne vinegar
1 tablespoon orange liqueur
Salt and pepper

1 tablespoon chopped fresh chives, for serving

Fish and Shellfish

Salmon Salad with Orange-Balsamic Dressing

Salmon is an ideal fish for the grill because of its firm, moist texture, and relatively high oil content, which means it is easier to cook without drying out. Dill is a natural partner for salmon, and its subtle flavor in the rub and the salad is the perfect touch.

PREP TIME: 15 mins ★ COOK TIME: 10 mins ★ GRILL TIME: 6 mins ★ SERVES 4

For the Salmon:
1/2 cup light brown sugar
1 tablespoon ground cumin
1/2 tablespoon pure red chile powder
1 teaspoon ground dill seed
1 teaspoon coarse salt
1/2 teaspoon freshly ground black pepper
4 skinless salmon fillets, about 5 ounces each

For the Salad:
2 cups freshly squeezed orange juice
2 teaspoons light brown sugar
2 tablespoons balsamic vinegar
3 tablespoons extra-virgin olive oil
Salt and pepper
2 Roma tomatoes, seeded and diced
2 teaspoons snipped fresh dill
2 1/2 cups arugula (about 3 ounces)
2 1/2 cups mesclun greens (about 3 ounces)

1 For the Salmon, place the brown sugar, cumin, chile powder, dill seed, salt, and pepper in a small bowl and mix well. Rub the salmon with the spice mixture. Place in a single layer in a glass baking dish. Cover and refrigerate 2 to 3 hours.

2 For the Salad, combine the orange juice and brown sugar in a small saucepan. Heat over medium-high heat until reduced to about 1/2 cup. Transfer to a medium mixing bowl and let cool. Add the vinegar and slowly add the oil, whisking until blended. Season with salt and pepper to taste. Whisk dressing again just before serving. Toss together the tomatoes and dill and set aside.

3 Preheat and oil the grill. Grill the salmon over direct medium-high heat about 3 minutes on each side for medium, 4 minutes on each side for medium-well.

4 Place the arugula and mesclun greens in a large bowl and drizzle with dressing. Toss to mix and season with salt and pepper to taste. Divide the greens among 4 plates. Top each salad with a piece of salmon and garnish with the tomato mixture. Serve right away.

Chef's Tip: Steaks or Fillets?

What's the difference between fish steaks and fillets? It's all about how the fish was cut up. For steaks, fish are cut crosswise and often include a piece of the backbone. Fillets are cut from the sides of each fish and are usually boneless. The cooking times for fish steaks are about the same as for thick fillets (such as from halibut or salmon) and can often be swapped in recipes; thin fillets, such as tilapia or striped bass, cook very quickly and cannot be used interchangably with fish steaks.

Herbed Halibut

Fresh herbs make all the difference in this recipe. The extra effort is worth the difference in flavor. Grilled Fennel (page 151) is a classic flavor partner for the mild halibut.

PREP TIME: 5 mins ★ GRILL TIME: 6 mins ★ SERVES 4

1 Preheat and oil the grill. Combine the herbs in a medium shallow bowl. Season with cayenne, salt, and pepper to taste, tossing to blend well.

2 Lightly brush both sides of the halibut fillets with olive oil. Press both sides of the fish into the herb mixture to coat.

3 Grill over direct medium-high heat about 3 minutes on each side, or until cooked through. Serve hot with lemon wedges.

> $\frac{1}{2}$ cup chopped fresh thyme
>
> $\frac{1}{2}$ cup chopped fresh oregano
>
> $\frac{1}{2}$ cup chopped fresh flat-leaf parsley
>
> Cayenne pepper
>
> Salt and pepper
>
> 4 halibut fillets, about 6 ounces each
>
> $\frac{1}{4}$ cup olive oil
>
> Lemon wedges, for serving

Brook Trout with Herb Butter

This is so easy to put together and always makes a great impression. If you prefer, you can have the trout butterflied (the head and bones will be removed, but the skin will keep the fillets attached to each other). Butterflied fillets cook a little faster; keep that in mind so they don't dry out.

PREP TIME: **5** mins ★ COOK TIME: **5** mins ★ GRILL TIME: **10** mins ★ SERVES **4**

½ cup unsalted butter

1 teaspoon freshly squeezed lemon juice

1 tablespoon chopped fresh flat-leaf parsley

1 teaspoon chopped fresh chives

Salt and pepper

4 whole trout, cleaned

1 Preheat and oil the grill. Melt the butter in a small skillet over low heat. Cook, stirring frequently, about 3 minutes or until the butter begins to foam. Cook just until it turns golden brown, watching so it doesn't burn. Immediately remove the skillet from the heat and stir in the lemon juice, parsley, and chives. Season with salt and pepper to taste. Keep warm while the fish grills.

2 Season the trout with salt and pepper to taste. Grill about 4 minutes or until the skin starts to char. Turn carefully, keeping the fish whole, and grill 5 minutes longer or until cooked through. Remove the fish from the grill, drizzle with butter, and serve.

Whole Grill-Roasted Salmon with New Potatoes and Leeks

Keep in mind when seasoning the fish that the bacon will add saltiness.

PREP TIME: 20 mins ★ GRILL TIME: 45 mins ★ SERVES 4

1 Preheat the grill. Season the inside of the salmon with salt and pepper to taste. Place the rosemary and lemon slices in the salmon cavity. Wrap the bacon around the salmon, completely covering the fish.

2 Spread the potatoes and leeks in a single layer in the bottom of an aluminum baking pan. Season with pepper to taste. Place the fish on top of the vegetables and potatoes. Place the pan on the grill rack, cover, and roast about 45 minutes, or until an instant-read thermometer reads 135°F when inserted into the thickest part of the salmon.

3 Remove the pan from the grill and let rest 15 minutes. Transfer fish and vegetables to a serving platter. Serve with lemon wedges.

One 4-to-5 pound salmon, cleaned, head and tail on

Salt and pepper

3 sprigs fresh rosemary

1 lemon, thinly sliced crosswise

½ pound sliced bacon (about 6 strips)

1 pound tiny new potatoes, cooked

4 leeks, white part only, washed well and cut in half lengthwise

Lemon wedges, for serving

Chef's Tip: How to Fillet a Fish

It may take a little practice, but filleting a whole fish at the table is always a good way to impress your guests. A sharp fillet knife (a knife with a thin 6-inch blade) is a must for clean-looking fillets. Place the fillet knife just behind the gill, the ngle the knife slightly downward until you feel the blade hit the fish's backbone. Turn the knife so it is parallel to the bone. Grasp the top fillet with your fingers and slowly run the knife down the length of the fish, from head to tail, lifting off the top fillet as you go. Angle a fork and the fillet knife under the bones and lift them up and away from the bottom fillet.

Grilled Whole Fish

A large firm-fleshed fish such as red snapper, branzino, or striped bass is best for grilling; it will stay moist even with the high heat of the grill.

PREP TIME: 5 mins ★ GRILL TIME: 20 mins ★ SERVES 4

One whole red snapper, about
    4 pounds, cleaned

Salt and pepper

A generous handful of fresh
    thyme, oregano, or rosemary
    (or a mix)

1 lemon, sliced crosswise

1 Preheat and oil the grill. Season the fish inside and out with salt and pepper to taste. Fill the cavity with herbs and lemon slices.

2 Grill the fish 10 minutes or until the flesh begins to firm up and the skin is charred. Carefully turn and grill the other side 10 minutes or until just cooked through. Remove from the grill and let rest 10 minutes before serving.

Chef's Tip: Fish Baskets

The tricky part of grilling a whole fish is keeping it whole when you turn it. We recommend using a wide fish spatula (page 13) or a fish-grilling basket. Fish baskets are made with the handle at one end or with a handle on the side (left). Either one is simple to use and makes turning the fish much easier. Spray the basket with cooking spray before using (even if it's a nonstick one).

Tuna Steaks with Hollandaise Sauce

This is an elegant dish and very easy to prepare. The hollandaise is a simple version of the classic sauce and goes well with nearly any grilled fish, chicken, or vegetable.

PREP TIME: **5 mins** ★ COOK TIME: **10 mins** ★ GRILL TIME: **6 mins** ★ SERVES **4**

1 Preheat and oil the grill. Melt the butter over medium heat in a small saucepan or in the microwave until hot but not bubbling. Place the egg yolks, lemon juice, orange juice, and hot pepper sauce and salt to taste in a blender. Process until well blended. With the motor on high, slowly add the hot butter in a steady stream, processing until thick. Scrape from the blender into the top half of a double boiler set over hot water and keep warm.

2 Season both sides of the tuna with salt and pepper to taste. Grill over direct medium-high heat about 3 minutes on each side for medium-rare or to the desired degree of doneness.

3 Remove tuna from the grill and serve with the sauce spooned over the top. Sprinkle with chopped parsley and serve.

½ cup unsalted butter

3 large egg yolks

2 teaspoons freshly squeezed lemon juice, strained

1 teaspoon freshly squeezed orange juice, strained

Hot pepper sauce

Salt and pepper

4 center-cut tuna steaks, about 8 ounces each and 1 inch thick

1 tablespoon chopped fresh flat-leaf parsley, for serving

Tuna Steaks with Mango-Chile Sauce

Grilled tuna steak has a softness and richness that's a little like filet mignon. Tuna's flavor is best when it's cooked medium-rare, but even if you prefer it cooked through, you will love it combined with this fruity, spicy sauce. The sauce also works well with seafood, pork, and chicken.

PREP TIME: 5 mins ★ GRILL TIME: 6 mins ★ SERVES 4

4 center-cut tuna steaks, about 8 ounces each and 1 inch thick

2 tablespoons grapeseed or peanut oil

1 teaspoon sweet paprika

½ teaspoon coarse salt

½ teaspoon freshly ground white pepper

Mango-Chile Sauce (page 27)

1 Preheat and oil the grill. Brush both sides of the tuna steaks with oil. Season with paprika, salt, and pepper.

2 Grill the tuna over direct medium-high heat about 3 minutes on each side for medium-rare or to the desired degree of doneness.

3 Cut each tuna steak crosswise into ½-inch slices, keeping each steak together. Spoon the sauce onto 4 plates and fan the tuna on top of the sauce. Serve right away.

Chef's Tip: Wood Plank Grilling

Grilling on a wooden plank combines the ease of a grill pan with the flavor-producing qualities of wood chips. Cedar is the most commonly used wood, but alder, oak, maple, cherry, and apple are all excellent choices for plank grilling. (You can buy wood planks especially for cooking in specialty food stores or online.) Cover the plank with water and soak at least 1 hour before using it so it does not catch on fire (if it does start to flame, spray it with water). Lightly brush the cooking side of the board with oil and arrange the food to be cooked in a single layer. Because you are cooking over indirect heat, plan for 50% longer cooking times than for direct grilling.

Clams with Herb Dipping Sauce

Clams are easy to do on the grill and are great outdoor-party food.
Whether you cook the larger or smaller number of clams, you will have plenty of sauce.

PREP TIME: **10 mins** ★ GRILL TIME: **10 mins** ★ SERVES **4**

1 Preheat and oil the grill. Combine the parsley, chives, basil, cilantro, and orange and lemon zest and juice in the bowl of a food processor fitted with a metal blade. Pulse until coarsely chopped and blended. Transfer mixture to a small serving bowl. Whisk in just enough oil to make a sauce. Season with salt to taste and set aside.

2 Place the clams on the grill with the flatter side down to keep the juices in. Cover and grill over direct medium-high heat about 10 minutes or until the clams open.

3 Remove from the grill and serve with the sauce for dipping.

Leaves from 1 bunch fresh
  flat-leaf parsley
1/2 cup chopped fresh chives
1/2 cup fresh basil leaves
1/2 cup fresh cilantro leaves
Freshly grated zest of 1 orange
Freshly grated zest of 1 lemon
2 tablespoons freshly squeezed
  orange juice
1 tablespoon freshly squeezed
  lemon juice
1 cup extra-virgin olive oil
Salt
40 to 60 clams in the shell

Barbecued Sea Scallops with Pineapple Salsa

Barbecued Sea Scallops with Pineapple Salsa

Couscous tossed with sliced scallions is a quick and easy side dish that complements the rich flavor of the scallops.

PREP TIME: 10 mins ★ GRILL TIME: 4 mins ★ SERVES 4

1 For the Scallops, place them in a single layer in a glass baking dish. Cover with the barbecue sauce. Cover and refrigerate 2 hours, turning the scallops after the first hour.

2 For the Salsa, combine the pineapple, bell pepper, onion, cilantro, and lime juice in a small bowl and toss to mix. Cover and refrigerate 2 hours.

3 Preheat and oil the grill. Remove the scallops from the sauce (discard sauce) and grill them over direct medium-high heat 2 to 3 minutes on each side or until cooked through. Serve with the pineapple salsa.

For the Scallops:
16 to 20 sea scallops, about 1½ pounds, rinsed and patted dry
1 cup Original Barbecue Sauce (page 28) or prepared barbecue sauce

For the Pineapple Salsa:
½ cup peeled, cored, and diced fresh pineapple
½ cup seeded and diced red bell pepper
½ cup minced red onion
1 tablespoon minced fresh cilantro
Juice of ½ lime

Grilled Citrusy Scallops

For an even quicker version of this recipe, you can marinate the scallops in plain orange juice for half an hour while the grill heats.

PREP TIME: 5 mins ★ GRILL TIME: 4 mins ★ SERVES 4

1 Whisk together the orange juice, honey, and vinegar in a medium bowl. Gradually whisk in the oil, then whisk in the lemon juice and orange zest. Place the scallops in a single layer in a glass baking dish. Cover and refrigerate 1 hour, turning the scallops after 30 minutes.

2 Preheat and oil the grill. Remove the scallops from the marinade (discard marinade) and grill them over direct medium-high heat 2 to 3 minutes on each side, or until cooked through.

½ cup freshly squeezed orange juice
½ cup honey
½ cup cider vinegar
½ cup olive oil
Juice of 1 lemon
Freshly grated zest of 1 orange
16 to 20 sea scallops, about 1½ pounds, rinsed and patted dry

Barbecued Shrimp

Leaving the shells on helps the hoisin sauce add flavor to the shrimp without overpowering them.

PREP TIME: **5 mins** ★ GRILL TIME: **5 mins** ★ SERVES **4**

½ cup hoisin sauce

½ cup freshly squeezed orange juice

½ cup rice wine vinegar

1 tablespoon "lite" soy sauce

1 teaspoon grated fresh ginger

2 pounds (about 15 per pound) shell-on jumbo shrimp

1 Combine the hoisin, orange juice, vinegar, soy sauce, and ginger in a large resealable plastic bag. Add the shrimp, seal, and knead the bag to coat. Refrigerate 1 hour.

2 Preheat and oil the grill. Remove the shrimp from the marinade (discard marinade) and grill, turning frequently, about 5 minutes or until curled and cooked through and pink. Remove from the grill and serve hot.

Sweet and Spicy Shrimp with Passion Fruit Sauce

You can use skewers if you don't have a perforated grill pan.
Put 3 or 4 shrimp on each skewer; the grilling time is the same.

PREP TIME: **10 mins** ★ GRILL TIME: **6 mins** ★ SERVES **4**

1 **For the Shrimp,** whisk together the brown sugar, lime juice, olive oil, cayenne, and salt in a medium bowl. Add the shrimp and toss to coat. Cover and refrigerate 30 minutes.

2 **For the Sauce,** melt the butter in a medium saucepan over medium heat and add the shallot, ginger, and garlic. Sauté 3 or 4 minutes and add the passion fruit puree. Bring to a simmer and reduce the heat to low. Cook 5 minutes, then strain into a clean pan; keep warm.

3 Preheat and oil the grill. Remove the shrimp from the marinade (discard marinade) and place on a perforated grill pan. Grill over direct medium-high heat 2 to 3 minutes on each side, or until the shrimp are cooked through and pink. Remove the shrimp from the grill and serve with the warm sauce.

For the Shrimp:
- 1/2 cup light brown sugar
- 2 tablespoons freshly squeezed lime juice
- 2 tablespoons olive oil
- 1/2 tablespoon cayenne pepper, or to taste
- 1/2 teaspoon coarse salt
- 1 1/2 pounds (about 15 per pound) jumbo shrimp, peeled and deveined

For the Sauce:
- 1 tablespoon unsalted butter
- 1 tablespoon minced shallot
- 1 tablespoon minced fresh ginger
- 1/2 tablespoon minced garlic
- 1/2 cup passion fruit puree

Chef's Tip: Fruit Purees

Exotic fruit purees like the passion fruit puree used in this recipe are sold at specialty food stores or online (check out perfectpuree.com). You can find lots of flavors, from unusual fruits like guava and prickly pear to more familiar flavors like blueberry and white peach. They are a quick and easy way to add real fruit flavor to sauces and marinades, or as an ingredient in frozen desserts or fruit smoothies.

Lobster Tails with Lemon-Lime Butter

It's important to use skewers to hold the lobster tails straight so they cook evenly. Push one through the meat of each tail, running from tip to tip, before cooking.

PREP TIME: 10 mins ★ GRILL TIME: 10 mins ★ SERVES 4

½ cup unsalted butter

1 tablespoon freshly squeezed lemon juice

1 tablespoon freshly squeezed lime juice

1 tablespoon chopped fresh basil

1 teaspoon chopped fresh chives

Salt and pepper

4 lobster tails (about 6 ounces each)

2 tablespoons peanut oil

1 Preheat and oil the grill. Heat the butter in a small saucepan over low heat until melted. Cook, stirring frequently, for about 3 minutes or until butter begins to foam, watching that it doesn't burn. Remove the pan from from the heat and stir in the citrus juices and herbs. Season with salt and pepper to taste. Set aside and keep warm while the lobster grills.

2 Push skewers lengthwise through the lobster tails. Rub the shells with oil and grill about 10 minutes or just until cooked through. Remove from the grill and serve with the warm butter for dipping.

Burgers and Kabobs

Texas Barbeque Bacon Burgers

We can't think of a better combination: hearty ground beef, crispy bacon, gooey cheese, and sweet onions, all topped with a spicy and smoky barbecue sauce. What more could you want?

PREP TIME: 10 mins ★ COOK TIME: 12 mins ★ GRILL TIME: 10 mins ★ SERVES 4

---

1 pound lean ground beef

1 tablespoon pure red chile powder, or to taste

Salt

12 slices bacon

1 red onion, sliced into ¼-inch-thick rings

4 kaiser rolls, split in half

4 (2-ounce) slices Cheddar cheese

1 cup Original Barbecue Sauce (see page 28) or bottled barbecue sauce

---

1 Preheat and oil the grill.

2 Combine the ground beef and chile powder in a medium bowl. Season with salt to taste and, using your hands, mix just until blended. Form the mixture into 4 patties about ½ inch thick.

3 Cook the bacon in a large skillet over medium heat about 8 minutes or until crispy. Transfer to a paper-towel-lined plate to drain. Pour off all but 1 tablespoon bacon drippings and return the skillet to the heat. Add the onion and sauté about 4 minutes or until soft and slightly golden.

4 Grill the patties over direct medium-high heat 5 to 6 minutes on each side or until medium and the internal temperature reaches 160°F. Meanwhile, toast the rolls over indirect medium heat about 5 minutes or until golden brown. Just before the patties are done, top each with a slice of Cheddar and cover the grill until the cheese is melted, about 1 minute.

5 Remove patties from the grill and let them rest 3 minutes. Meanwhile, heat the barbecue sauce over medium heat just until warm.

6 Spread the cut sides of the rolls with barbecue sauce. Top with a burger, then onion, bacon, and the tops of the rolls. Serve remaining barbecue sauce on the side.

High Thyme Burgers

These are great fall burgers with the scents of thyme and sage, evocative of the great outdoors.

PREP TIME: 10 mins ★ GRILL TIME: 10 mins ★ SERVES 4

1 Preheat and oil the grill.

2 Combine the ground meat, spinach, onion, parsley, thyme, sage, and orange zest, stirring to blend. Add the breadcrumbs and, using your hands, mix well. Season with salt and pepper to taste and form the mixture into 4 patties about ½ inch thick.

3 Grill the patties over direct medium-high heat 5 to 6 minutes per side or until medium and the internal temperature reaches 160°F. Meanwhile, toast the bread over indirect medium heat until golden brown, about 5 minutes.

4 Remove patties from the grill and let them rest 3 minutes. Serve on the toasted bread with the condiments of your choice.

12 ounces ground sirloin
12 ounces ground chuck
1 cup thawed frozen chopped spinach, very well drained
½ cup minced onion
1 tablespoon chopped fresh flat-leaf parsley
1 teaspoon ground dried thyme
½ teaspoon ground dried sage
½ teaspoon freshly grated orange zest
½ cup seasoned bread crumbs
Salt and pepper
4 (3-inch) pieces Italian bread, cut in half horizontally

Mushroom Swiss Burgers

*Make these burgers even more decadent by sautéing ¼ cup chopped pancetta
in the butter before adding the mushrooms.*

PREP TIME: 10 mins ★ COOK TIME: 8 mins ★ GRILL TIME: 10 mins ★ SERVES 4

1 pound ground beef
Salt and pepper
2 tablespoons unsalted butter
2 cups sliced mixed wild
   mushrooms
4 kaiser rolls, split in half
4 slices Swiss cheese
4 tablespoons mayonnaise

1 Preheat and oil the grill.

2 Season the ground beef with salt and pepper to taste. Using your hands, mix well and form into 4 patties about ½ inch thick.

3 Meanwhile, melt butter in a medium skillet over medium heat. Add mushrooms and cook, stirring, until cooked through and lightly browned, about 5 minutes. Season with salt and pepper to taste and keep warm.

4 Grill the patties over direct medium-high heat 5 to 6 minutes on each side or until medium and the internal temperature reaches 160°F. Just before the patties are done, top each with a slice of cheese and cover the grill about 1 minute, or until the cheese is melted. Meanwhile, toast the rolls over indirect medium heat about 5 minutes, or until golden brown.

5 Remove patties from the grill and let them rest 3 minutes. Spread mayonnaise on the bottom half of each kaiser roll. Top each with a patty, and ¼ cup mushrooms, and the top of a roll.

Maytag Blue Cheese Burgers

Maytag is a blue-veined cheese produced in Iowa that ranks up there with other world-class blues. Does the name sound familiar? Yes, it is from the same family that makes washing machines!

PREP TIME: 10 mins ★ GRILL TIME: 10 mins ★ SERVES 4

1 Preheat and oil the grill.

2 Combine the ground beef with the garlic, onion, parsley, Worcestershire sauce, and Tabasco sauce in a medium bowl. Season with salt and pepper to taste, and, using your hands, mix well and form into 4 balls. Poke a hole into the center of each ball and insert the cheese. Wrap the beef around the cheese and gently flatten to make 4 patties about ½ inch thick.

3 Grill the patties over direct medium-high heat 5 to 6 minutes on each side or until medium and the internal temperature reaches 160°F. Meanwhile, toast the buns over indirect medium heat about 5 minutes, or until golden brown.

4 Remove patties from the grill and let them rest 4 minutes. Place the lettuce and tomato on the bottom half of each hamburger bun. Add the patties and the top of each bun.

- 1½ pounds lean ground beef
- 2 cloves garlic, minced
- 2 tablespoons minced onion
- 1 tablespoon minced fresh flat-leaf parsley
- ½ teaspoon Worcestershire sauce
- ½ teaspoon Tabasco sauce
- Salt and freshly ground black pepper
- 2 ounces Maytag Blue cheese, cut into 4 cubes
- 4 whole wheat hamburger buns, split in half
- 4 lettuce leaves
- 4 tomato slices, about ½ inch thick

Chef's Tip: How to Stuff a Burger

The trick to stuffing a burger with cheese is to make sure the cheese is completely sealed in the ground meat. Any cracks or gaps in the patty will cause the cheese to melt and ooze out. When stuffing these burgers, place the cheese in the very center of the patty and wrap the meat completely around it. You can use this method with other soft cheeses, such as feta or goat cheese.

Burgers with Caramelized Onions

A little Worcestershire sauce enhances the flavor of beef in this recipe that will appeal to all burger fans. The caramelized onions are also excellent on steaks.

PREP TIME: 25 mins ★ GRILL TIME: 10 mins ★ SERVES 4

For the Onions:
1 tablespoon olive oil
1 tablespoon unsalted butter
2 sweet onions, very finely
  sliced
2 cloves garlic, minced
$\frac{1}{2}$ teaspoon coarse salt
$\frac{1}{8}$ teaspoon freshly ground
  black pepper
2 tablespoons sherry vinegar
  or beef broth
2 tablespoons brown sugar

For the Burgers:
$1\frac{1}{2}$ pounds lean ground beef
1 tablespoon Worcestershire
  sauce (optional), or to taste
Salt and freshly ground black
  pepper
4 hamburger buns or Kaiser
  rolls, split in half
4 tablespoons Red Pepper Aioli
  (see page 91)

1 Preheat and oil the grill.

2 **For the Onions,** heat the oil and butter in a medium skillet over medium heat. Add the onions and garlic. Season with salt and pepper and sauté over medium-high heat 10 to 12 minutes, stirring often, or until the onions are browned and caramelized. Add the vinegar and brown sugar and cook 5 minutes longer, or until the liquid has evaporated and the onions are just moist.

3 **For the Burgers,** combine the ground beef and the Worcestershire sauce in a medium bowl. Season with salt and pepper to taste. Using your hands, mix until blended. Form into 4 patties about $\frac{1}{2}$ inch thick.

4 Grill the patties over direct medium-high heat 5 to 6 minutes on each side or until medium and the internal temperature reaches 160°F. Meanwhile, toast the buns over indirect medium heat until golden brown, about 5 minutes.

5 Remove patties from the grill and let them rest 4 minutes. Spread about $\frac{1}{2}$ tablespoon aioli on the bottom half of each bun. Add the patties and the top of each bun.

Firecracker Burgers with Lime Mayo

These burgers have a real kick, but the Lime Mayo keeps the heat in check.
Sweet potato chips or fries would be an ideal accompaniment to the spicy burgers and tangy sauce.

PREP TIME: 10 mins ★ GRILL TIME: 10 mins ★ SERVES 4

1 For the Mayo, combine mayonnaise, yogurt, lime juice and zest, and ½ teaspoon salt in a small bowl; set aside.

2 For the Burgers, preheat and oil the grill. Combine ground beef, curry powder, jerk seasoning, and remaining ¾ teaspoon salt in a large bowl. Using your hands, mix just until blended. Shape into 4 patties about ¾ inch thick.

3 Grill the patties over direct medium-high heat 5 to 6 minutes on each side or until medium and the internal temperature reaches 160°F. Meanwhile, toast the buns over indirect medium heat until golden brown, about 5 minutes.

4 Remove patties from the grill and let them rest 3 minutes. Spread 2 tablespoons Lime Mayo on the cut sides of each bun. Place a burger on bottom half of each bun, top with watercress, and serve.

For the Lime Mayo:
½ cup mayonnaise
¼ cup plain yogurt
1 tablespoon freshly squeezed lime juice
2 teaspoons freshly grated lime zest
1¼ teaspoons salt

For the Firecracker Burgers:
1½ pounds lean ground beef
1 tablespoon curry powder
1 tablespoon Caribbean jerk seasoning
4 sesame seed buns, split in half horizontally
1 cup watercress, washed and dried

Chile Burgers with Salsa Fresca

Here is a classic burger with a little Tex-Mex twist! You can make both the burgers and the salsa as hot or as mild as you wish by adjusting the amount of chile you add.

PREP TIME: 10 mins ★ GRILL TIME: 10 mins ★ SERVES 4

12 ounces ground sirloin

12 ounces ground chuck

½ cup minced red bell pepper

½ cup minced red onion

1 tablespoon pure red chile
    powder

½ teaspoon ground cumin

Salt and pepper

4 (8-inch) flour tortillas

1 cup Salsa Fresca (page 53)

1 Preheat and oil the grill.

2 Combine the ground meat, bell pepper, onion, chile powder, and cumin. Season with salt and pepper to taste. Using your hands, mix thoroughly. Form the mixture into 4 patties about ½ inch thick.

3 Grill the patties over direct medium-high heat 5 to 6 minutes on each side, or until the internal temperature reaches 160°F. Wrap the tortillas in foil and heat over indirect medium-high heat until warm, about 5 minutes.

4 Remove patties from the grill and let them rest 3 minutes. Wrap each patty in a tortilla and top with salsa.

Kona Burgers

Kona coffee from Hawaii's Big Island really perks up these burgers, giving them an unexpected and delicious flavor (and don't worry, they won't keep you up at night). You can substitute good-quality espresso for the Kona coffee, if you prefer.

PREP TIME: 10 mins ★ GRILL TIME: 10 mins ★ SERVES 4

1 Preheat and oil the grill.

2 Combine the ground beef, garlic, onion, 2 tablespoons of the olive oil, and salt. Using your hands, mix well and form into 4 patties about ½ inch thick. Mix the ground coffee and pepper on a plate. Press both sides of each burger into the mixture so they are well coated.

3 Brush the patties with the remaining 1 tablespoon olive oil. Grill over direct medium-high heat 5 to 6 minutes on each side, or until medium and the internal temperature reaches 160°F. Meanwhile, toast the buns over indirect medium heat about 5 minutes, or until golden brown.

4 Remove patties from the grill and let them rest 3 minutes. Place the lettuce and tomato on the bottom half of each bun. Add a patty and the top half of a bun to each. Serve with the condiments of your choice.

1½ pounds lean ground beef
2 cloves garlic, minced
½ cup minced red onion
3 tablespoons olive oil, divided
1 tablespoon coarse salt
2 tablespoons freshly ground pure Kona coffee
1 tablespoon freshly ground black pepper
4 whole wheat hamburger buns, split in half horizontally
4 lettuce leaves
4 tomato slices, about ½ inch thick

Chef's Tip: About Kona Coffee

Kona coffee is the market name for a variety of coffee grown in the Kona *mokus,* or districts, of the Big Island of Hawaii. Only coffee grown there can be sold under the name "Kona."

Hail Caesar Burgers

Add anchovy fillets, if you like, for traditional Caesar flavor.

PREP TIME: 10 mins ★ GRILL TIME: 10 mins ★ SERVES 4

1 cup shredded Parmesan cheese

1 tablespoon freshly ground black pepper

2 pita breads, cut in half to make 4 pockets

1½ cups prepared Caesar dressing

1 pound lean ground beef

4 romaine hearts, torn into bite-sized pieces

1 Preheat and oil the grill.

2 Combine the ground beef, ½ cup shredded Parmesan, and black pepper in a medium bowl. Using your hands, mix just until blended. Form the mixture 4 patties about ½ inch thick.

3 Grill the patties over direct medium-high heat 5 to 6 minutes on each side or until medium and the internal temperature reaches 160°F. Wrap the pita in foil and warm on the edgeof the grill 3 minutes. Just before the patties are done, sprinkle each with 1 tablespoon Parmesan. Cover and grill about 1 minute, or until the cheese is softened.

4 Remove patties from the grill and let them rest 3 minutes. Toss the romaine with the Caesar dressing and divide evenly among the pita pockets. Add a burger to each, sprinkle with remaining Parmesan, and serve.

Chef's Tip: Simple Caesar Dressing

No need to buy bottled dressing—you probably have the ingredients on hand. Adjust the amounts to your own tastes. (The anchovy paste is optional; if you decide to omit it, you may need to add a little salt.) Combine 2 tablespoons freshly squeezed lemon juice, 2 tablespoons freshly grated Parmesan cheese, 1 tablespoon olive oil, 1 tablespoon warm water, 1 teaspoon Dijon mustard, 1 teaspoon Worcestershire sauce, 1 teaspoon minced garlic, and 1 teaspoon anchovy paste (if desired) in the container of a blender. Puree until smooth. Transfer to a medium bowl and whisk in 1 cup mayonnaise. Season with ground black pepper to taste. Cover and regrigerate until serving.

Italian Sausage Burgers

You can use sausage links for these burgers; just remove the casings before mixing the sausage with the ground sirloin. Top the cooked burgers with sautéed onions and red and green bell peppers for the full Brooklyn street-fair experience.

PREP TIME: 5 mins ★ GRILL TIME: 10 mins ★ SERVES 4

12 ounces ground beef sirloin

6 ounces hot Italian sausage meat

4 ounces sweet Italian sausage meat

Salt and pepper

1 tablespoon chopped fresh flat-leaf parsley

4 Italian rolls, split and toasted

1 cup marinara sauce, warmed

1 Preheat and oil the grill.

2 Combine the ground sirloin and sausages in a medium bowl. Season with salt and pepper to taste, add the parsley, and, using your hands, mix thoroughly. Form the mixture into 4 patties about ½ inch thick.

3 Grill the patties over direct medium-high heat 5 to 6 minutes on each side or until medium and the internal temperature reaches 160°F. Meanwhile, toast the rolls over indirect medium heat about 5 minutes, or until golden brown.

4 Remove patties from the grill and let them rest 3 minutes. Place the patties on the bottom half of each toasted roll, spoon some of the marinara sauce over, cover with the tops of the rolls, and serve.

BBQ Pork Burgers

This easy alternative to pulled-pork sandwiches is a terrific addition to any backyard barbecue. An iceberg wedge with ranch or blue cheese dressing is our favorite partner.

PREP TIME: 10 mins ★ GRILL TIME: 10 mins ★ SERVES 4

1 Preheat and oil the grill. Combine the onion and pickles in a small bowl and set aside.

2 Combine the ground pork and ½ cup of the barbecue sauce. Season with salt and pepper to taste and, using your hands, mix thoroughly. Form the mixture into 4 oblong patties about ½ inch thick.

3 Grill the patties over direct medium-high heat about 5 minutes on each side or until medium-well and the internal temperature reaches 160°F. Meanwhile, toast the hot dog buns over indirect medium heat about 5 minutes, or until golden brown.

4 Remove the patties from the grill and let them rest 3 minutes. Place the patties on the toasted buns, top with the onion and pickle mixture, and serve with the remaining barbecue sauce on the side.

> 1 cup chopped red onion
> ½ cup chopped sweet pickles
> 1½ pounds ground pork
> 1 cup Original Barbecue Sauce (page 28), or bottled barbecue sauce
> Salt and pepper
> 4 large hot dog buns, split in half

Curried Chicken Burgers

These flavorful burgers are a delicious departure from the everyday.
Serve with Spiced Waldorf Salad (page 161).

PREP TIME: 10 mins ★ GRILL TIME: 10 mins ★ SERVES 4

1½ pounds ground chicken

1 tablespoon minced fresh cilantro

1 tablespoon curry powder

1 teaspoon minced garlic

½ teaspoon ground cumin

½ teaspoon freshly grated orange zest

½ cup chopped prepared chutney, plus more for serving

Salt and pepper

4 warm pita breads, split to make pockets

⅓ cup chopped hothouse cucumber

⅓ cup chopped spinach leaves

1 Preheat and oil the grill.

2 Combine the ground chicken, cilantro, curry powder, garlic, cumin, and orange zest in a medium bowl. Using your hands, mix thoroughly. Add the chutney and season with salt and pepper to taste. Form the mixture into 4 patties about ½ inch thick.

3 Grill the patties over direct medium-high heat about 5 minutes on each side or until cooked through. Wrap the pita pockets in foil and warm on the edge of the grill 3 minutes.

4 Remove patties from the grill and let them rest 3 minutes. Place a burger in each pita pocket, top with the chopped cucumber and spinach. Serve with additional chutney on the side.

Spicy Chicken Burgers with Guacamole

The guacamole adds just the right amount of buttery smoothness to balance out the zesty flavor of the burgers. Be sure to have some tortilla chips on hand for dipping into any extra guacamole.

PREP TIME: 20 mins ★ GRILL TIME: 10 mins ★ SERVES 4

1 Preheat and oil the grill.

2 **For the Guacamole,** combine the avocados with the lime juice and tomatoes in a medium bowl and stir in the cilantro, scallion, and jalapeño. Season with salt and pepper to taste. Cover with plastic wrap pressed directly on the surface of the guacamole.

3 **For the Burgers,** combine the ground chicken with the egg white in a large bowl, using your hands to blend. Add the jalapeño, bell pepper, scallion, chile powder, and cumin. Again, using your hands, mix thoroughly. Season with salt and pepper to tasteand form the mixture into 4 patties, about ½ inch thick.

4 Grill the patties over direct medium-high heat about 5 minutes per side until cooked through. Wrap the tortillas in foil and warm on the edge of the grill 3 minutes.

5 Remove patties from the grill and let them rest 3 minutes. Wrap each patty in a tortilla and top with guacomole.

For the Guacamole:

2 avocados, peeled, pitted, and mashed

Juice of 1 lime

½ cup chopped tomatoes

2 tablespoons chopped fresh cilantro

2 tablespoons chopped scallion

1 teaspoon minced jalapeño chile, or to taste

Salt and pepper

For the Spicy Chicken Burgers:

1½ pounds ground chicken

1 large egg white

1 jalapeño, seeded and minced, or more to taste

3 tablespoons minced red bell pepper

2 tablespoons minced scallion

1 teaspoon pure red chile powder

½ teaspoon ground cumin

Salt and pepper

4 (8-inch) flour tortillas

Thanksgiving Turkey Burgers

These flavorful burgers are close to the real thing... and a lot easier! They're great for tailgate parties.

PREP TIME: 10 mins ★ GRILL TIME: 5 mins ★ SERVES 4

½ cup mayonnaise

3 tablespoons jellied cranberry sauce

1 tablespoon unsalted butter

½ cup minced onion

1 teaspoon chopped fresh sage

1 teaspoon fresh thyme leaves

1½ pounds ground turkey

1 large egg white

½ cup dried cranberries

½ cup crushed dry stuffing mix

Salt and pepper

4 hamburger buns, split in half

1 Preheat and oil the grill. Combine the mayonnaise and cranberry sauce in a small mixing bowl. Set aside.

2 Melt the butter in a small sauté pan set over medium heat. Add the onion, sage, and thyme; sauté about 3 minutes or until the onion is soft. Remove from the heat.

3 Combine the turkey and the egg white in a large bowl, using your hands to blend. Add the cranberries, onion mixture, and stuffing mix and mix thoroughly. Season with salt and pepper to taste and form the mixture into 4 patties about ½ inch thick.

4 Grill the patties over direct medium-high heat about 5 minutes on each side or just until cooked through. Do not overcook; the turkey will dry out quickly. Meanwhile, toast the buns over indirect medium heat about 5 minutes, or until golden brown.

5 Remove patties from the grill and let them rest 3 minutes. Coat the cut sides of each bun with 2 tablespoons of the mayonnaise mixture, add the patties, and serve.

Pesto-Flavored Turkey Burgers

Store-bought pesto makes these interesting burgers a breeze to prepare.
It is available in the frozen-food section or Italian section of most supermarkets.

PREP TIME: 15 mins ★ GRILL TIME: 10 mins ★ SERVES 4

1 Preheat and oil the grill. Combine the mayonnaise and 2 tablespoons pesto in a small mixing bowl. Set aside.

2 Combine the turkey with the remaining ½ cup of the pesto in a large bowl, using your hands to blend. Add the lemon juice and mix thoroughly. Season with salt and pepper to taste, and form the mixture into 4 patties about ½ inch thick.

3 Grill the patties over direct medium-high heat about 5 minutes on each side or just until cooked through. Do not overcook; the turkey will dry out quickly. Meanwhile, toast the buns over indirect medium heat about 5 minutes, or until golden brown.

4 Remove patties from the grill and let them rest 3 minutes. Coat the cut sides of each bun with 2 tablespoons of the mayonnaise mixture, add the patties, top with arugula, and serve.

½ cup mayonnaise

½ cup plus 2 tablespoons store-bought pesto sauce, divided

1½ pounds ground turkey

1 tablespoon freshly squeezed lemon juice

Salt and pepper

4 hamburger buns, split in half

2 cups arugula leaves

Chef's Tip: Homemade Pesto

Combine ⅔ cup packed, coarsely chopped fresh basil, ⅓ cup grated Parmesan cheese, ⅓ cup extra-virgin olive oil, 2 tablespoons pine nuts, and 1 clove minced garlic in a food processor fitted with the metal blade. Pulse until a coarse puree forms. Season with salt and pepper to taste. To freeze pesto, just spoon it into a small freezer-safe container and cover the top surface with a thin layer of olive oil. Wrap tightly in plastic wrap and use within 3 months.

Salmon Burgers
with Herbed Tartar Sauce

The tartar sauce can be used with a wide variety of fish dishes, grilled and otherwise.

PREP TIME: 20 mins ★ GRILL TIME: 8 mins ★ SERVES 4

For the Herbed Tartar Sauce:
2 sweet pickles, chopped
1 large shallot, chopped
1 hard-boiled egg yolk
2 tablespoons chopped pitted
  green olives
1 teaspoon chopped capers
1 teaspoon chopped fresh
  flat-leaf parsley
1 teaspoon chopped fresh
  chives
1 teaspoon chopped fresh dill
1/2 cup mayonnaise
2 tablespoons sour cream
1 teaspoon Dijon mustard
Salt and pepper

For the Salmon Burgers:
1 pound chopped fresh salmon
6 ounces chopped smoked
  salmon
1 large egg yolk
1/2 cup finely diced red or
  yellow bell pepper
2 tablespoons Dijon mustard
1 tablespoon chopped fresh
  chives
1/2 cup fresh bread crumbs
Salt and pepper
1/2 cup olive oil
4 seeded rolls or hamburger
  buns, split in half

1 For the Tartar Sauce, combine the pickles, shallot, egg yolk, olives, capers, parsley, chives, and dill in the bowl of a food processor fitted with the metal blade. Pulse until finely chopped. Add the mayonnaise, sour cream, and mustard. Process until blended. Season with salt and pepper to taste. Transfer to a clean container, cover, and refrigerate until ready to use.

2 Preheat and oil the grill.

3 For the Burgers, combine the fresh salmon, smoked salmon, egg yolk, bell pepper, mustard, and chives in a large bowl, and mix until blended. Stir in the bread crumbs and season with salt and pepper to taste. Form the mixture into 4 patties about 1/2 inch thick.

4 Brush both sides of the patties with oil. Grill the patties over direct medium-high heat 4 to 5 minutes on each side. Meanwhile, toast the rolls over indirect medium heat about 5 minutes, or until golden brown.

5 Remove patties from the grill and place on the toasted rolls. Serve with the tartar sauce on the side.

Teriyaki Tuna Burgers

This is a great way to use the ends of fresh tuna steaks. These can usually be found at a substantially lower price per pound than sushi-grade tuna steaks. The teriyaki glaze also works well with chicken and pork.

PREP TIME: 10 mins ★ COOK TIME: 15 mins ★ GRILL TIME: 6 mins ★ SERVES 4

1 cup soy sauce

½ cup mirin (available in specialty food stores and Asian markets)

1 tablespoon honey

1 teaspoon toasted (dark) sesame oil

1 pound chopped fresh tuna

½ cup white sesame seeds, toasted

Salt and pepper

1 Preheat and oil the grill. Combine the soy sauce, mirin, honey, and sesame oil in a small saucepan and heat over medium heat. Bring to a simmer and cook, stirring constantly, about 12 minutes or until reduced by half and quite thick. Remove the pan from the heat.

2 Combine the tuna with the sesame seeds in a large bowl and, using your hands, mix until blended. Season with salt and pepper to taste and form into 4 patties about ½ inch thick. Lightly brush both sides of the patties with the glaze.

3 Grill the tuna patties, brushing frequently with the glaze, about 3 minutes on each side for medium or until cooked to the desired degree of doneness.

Chef's Tip: Toasting Sesame Seeds

Toasting enhances the nutty flavor of sesame seeds. Heat the sesame seeds in a single layer in a skillet over medium heat, shaking the pan occasionally, about 2 minutes or until the seeds darken slightly and become fragrant. Let cool completely before using.

Portobello Mushroom Burgers with Grilled Onions and Peppers

This is the most satisfying vegetarian burger we've tried, but feel free to add a hamburger patty for a triple-decker version.

PREP TIME: 10 MINS ★ GRILL TIME: 12 MINS ★ SERVES 4

1 Place the mushroom caps, onions, and bell peppers in a medium glass baking dish. Add the vinegar, oil, thyme, parsley, and salt and pepper to taste. Let stand at room temperature 1 hour. Preheat and oil the grill.

2 Remove the onions from the marinade and grill over direct medium-high heat for about 5 minutes, turning occasionally. Move the onions to the cooler part of the grill and add the mushrooms and peppers to the direct heat. Grill, turning occasionally, 5 minutes. Meanwhile, toast the rolls over indirect medium heat about 5 minutes, or until golden brown.

3 While the vegetables are grilling, heat the marinade in a small saucepan over low heat until warm.

4 Remove the vegetables from the grill. Place 1 mushroom cap on the bottom half of each of the 4 rolls. Top each with an onion half and 2 pieces of bell pepper. Drizzle with the warm marinade and add the top half of the rolls. Press down gently to allow the juices to soak into the rolls and serve.

> 4 large portobello mushroom caps
>
> 2 large onions, peeled and cut in half crosswise
>
> 2 red bell peppers, seeded and quartered
>
> 1 cup balsamic vinegar
>
> 1 cup extra-virgin olive oil
>
> 1 tablespoon minced fresh thyme
>
> 1 tablespoon minced fresh flat-leaf parsley
>
> Salt and pepper
>
> 4 crusty Italian rolls, split in half

Honey-Mustard Beef Kabobs

Use spicy mustard in place of the Dijon to add a little heat to these kabobs, if you like.

PREP TIME: **15 mins** ★ GRILL TIME: **15 mins** ★ SERVES **4**

For the Honey-Mustard Seasoning:

1 tablespoon freshly squeezed lemon juice

1 tablespoon olive oil

1 tablespoon water

2 teaspoons Dijon mustard

1 teaspoon honey

1/2 teaspoon dried oregano, crumbled

1/4 teaspoon ground black pepper

For the Beef Kabobs:

1 pound sirloin tips

1 large red, yellow, or green bell pepper, cut into 1 1/4-inch pieces

12 large button mushrooms

1/4 teaspoon salt

1 Preheat and oil the grill. Cover eight 12-inch bamboo skewers with water and let soak at least half an hour.

2 Whisk together the seasoning ingredients in a large bowl. Add the steak, bell pepper, and mushrooms, tossing to coat. Alternately thread pieces of steak, bell pepper, and mushroom onto each skewer, dividing ingredients evenly. Season with salt.

3 Grill over direct medium-high heat, turning frequently, about 7 minutes for medium-rare, 8 to 9 minutes for medium, or to the desired doneness. Let rest 3 minutes before serving.

Chef's Tip: Building Kabobs

You will notice that we direct you to alternate the protein used for the kabobs with the other ingredients, such as vegetables or fruit. The reason for this is that the juices from the non-protein ingredients serve to flavor and moisten the protein as it cooks on the grill. While you can swap vegetables as you like (such as using different colors of peppers or adding tomatoes, mushrooms, or onions), we don't suggest making kabobs with multiple proteins (unless one is already cooked, as in the Scallop and Ham Kabobs on page 140); or with just protein ingredients—the end result will not be as flavorful or juicy.

Marinated Beef Kabobs

*Use tiny heirloom potatoes for these kabobs. If they are not available,
you can cut cooked potatoes (we like Yukon Golds) into 1-inch cubes.*

PREP TIME: 20 mins ★ GRILL TIME: 15 mins ★ SERVES 4

1 cup balsamic vinegar

1/2 cup red wine

3 tablespoons extra-virgin
olive oil

1 tablespoon molasses or honey

2 tablespoons chopped fresh
rosemary

1 tablespoon chopped fresh
thyme

1 teaspoon cracked black
pepper

2 pounds filet mignon steaks,
cut into 24 1 1/2-inch cubes

8 frozen pearl onions, thawed,
drained, and patted dry

8 button mushroom caps

12 cooked new potatoes

Coarse salt

1 Stir together the vinegar, wine, olive oil, molasses, rosemary,
thyme, and pepper in a glass baking dish. Add the beef, onions,
and mushroom caps and toss to coat. Cover and refrigerate at
least 1 hour and up to 6 hours.

2 Preheat and oil the grill. Cover eight 12-inch bamboo
skewers with water and let soak at least half an hour.

3 Remove the beef and vegetables from the marinade; do
not discard the marinade. To build the skewers, alternate a
potato, a piece of meat, an onion, a piece of meat, and a
mushroom on each.

4 Brush each skewer with marinade and season with salt to
taste. Grill over direct medium-high heat, turning frequently,
about 7 minutes for medium-rare, 8 to 9 minutes for medium,
or to the desired doneness. Let rest for 3 minutes before serving.

Rosemary Chicken Kabobs

These are best done on skewers made from rosemary branches;
use metal or soaked bamboo skewers if you prefer.

PREP TIME: 20 mins ★ GRILL TIME: 10 mins ★ SERVES 4

1 Preheat and oil the grill. Combine the chicken, olive oil, lemon juice and zest, rosemary, and garlic in a large bowl. Season with salt and pepper to taste and let stand at room temperature 30 minutes.

2 To build the kabobs, start with chicken, then a tomato, then a pepper piece. Repeat 3 times for each kabob.

3 Brush each skewer with marinade and season with salt and pepper to taste. Grill, turning frequently, about 10 minutes or until cooked through. Remove from the grill and serve.

1½ pounds boneless, skinless chicken thighs or breasts, cut into ½-inch cubes

½ cup olive oil

½ cup freshly squeezed lemon juice

1 tablespoon freshly grated lemon zest

1 tablespoon chopped fresh rosemary

1 tablespoon minced garlic

Salt and pepper

24 cherry tomatoes

24 (1-inch squares) green bell pepper

8 sturdy branches rosemary

Hot and Sweet Italian Sausage Skewers

We have used both hot and sweet sausage for these skewers, but they can be made with all one kind.

PREP TIME: 15 mins ★ GRILL TIME: 6 mins ★ SERVES 4

16 (1-inch) squares red bell pepper

8 (1-inch) squares green bell pepper

16 button mushroom caps

1/2 cup extra-virgin olive oil

1/2 cup balsamic vinegar

Salt and pepper

16 (1-inch) pieces hot Italian sausage

16 (1-inch) pieces sweet Italian sausage

Warmed marinara sauce, for dipping

1 Combine the peppers and mushrooms in a shallow baking dish. Add the olive oil and vinegar, season with salt and pepper to taste, and toss to coat. Let stand at room temperature 30 minutes.

2 Preheat and oil the grill. Cover 8 bamboo skewers with water and soak for at least half an hour.

3 To build the skewers, alternate peppers and each kind of sausage with the mushrooms, dividing the ingredients evenly. Grill over direct medium-high heat, turning frequently, about 6 minutes or until the sausage is cooked through and the vegetables are crisp-tender. Serve with warm marinara sauce.

Lamb and Eggplant Skewers

You can use lamb loin instead of lamb shoulder in these kabobs.

PREP TIME: 20 mins ★ GRILL TIME: 7 mins ★ SERVES 4

1/2 cup extra-virgin olive oil

2 tablespoons minced fresh oregano

2 cloves garlic, minced

1 pound boneless shoulder of lamb, cut into 1-inch dice

1 small eggplant, about 12 ounces, cut into 1-inch dice

1 teaspoon coarse salt

1 red onion, cut into wedges

2 tablespoons olive oil

Freshly ground black pepper

1 Combine the olive oil, oregano, and garlic in a glass baking dish. Add the lamb and toss to coat. Cover and refrigerate 2 to 3 hours.

2 Preheat and oil the grill. Cover 8 bamboo skewers with water and let soak for at least half an hour.

3 Bring the lamb to room temperature. Place the eggplant in a colander, sprinkle with the salt, and set in the sink for 20 minutes to drain, turning once or twice. Rinse with cold water; let drain well. Pat the eggplant dry with paper towels. Brush the eggplant and onion with olive oil, and season with salt and pepper to taste. Build the skewers, alternating the lamb, eggplant, and onion. Grill over direct medium-high heat 7 or 8 minutes, turning occasionally, for medium-rare. Let the kabobs rest 3 minutes before serving.

Miso-Glazed Salmon Kabobs

This wonderful glaze works well with fish, shellfish, pork, or poultry. It is quite sweet—take care that it doesn't burn before the fish is cooked. Two skewers served with jasmine rice and some steamed edamame are a lovely light meal.

PREP TIME: 10 mins ★ COOK TIME: 5 mins ★ GRILL TIME: 6 mins ★ SERVES 4

---

2 cups sweet white miso

1/2 cup mirin

1/2 cup sake

1/2 cup plus 2 tablespoons light brown sugar

1 1/2 pounds boneless thick salmon fillet, cut into 1 1/2-inch cubes

16 frozen pearl onions, thawed, very well drained, and patted dry

---

1 Combine the miso, mirin, sake, and brown sugar in a small saucepan over medium heat. Bring to a simmer and immediately reduce the heat. Cook, stirring constantly, about 2 minutes or until the sugar has dissolved completely. Remove from the heat and set aside to cool.

2 Place the salmon in a glass baking dish. Add the glaze and toss to coat well. Cover and refrigerate 6 hours, tossing occasionally to ensure that all sides of the fish are coated with the glaze. Add the onions, cover, and refrigerate 6 hours longer.

3 Preheat and oil the grill. Cover 8 bamboo skewers with water and soak at least half an hour.

4 Remove the salmon and onions from the glaze, brushing off excess. Build the skewers, alternating 3 pieces of salmon and 2 onions on each. Grill, turning frequently, about 6 minutes for medium-rare or 8 minutes for medium, and the onions are glazed.

Tuna and Artichoke Brochettes

Marinating the tuna in this recipe helps keep it moist during cooking. For extra richness, serve Hollandaise Sauce (see page 101) on the side for dipping.

PREP TIME: 10 mins ★ GRILL TIME: 6 mins ★ SERVES 4

1 Place tuna in a single layer in a glass baking dish. Whisk together the olive oil, lemon juice, garlic, paprika, salt, and pepper to taste in a small bowl. Pour the mixture over the tuna, cover, and refrigerate 1 hour.

2 Preheat and oil the grill. Cover 12 bamboo skewers with water and soak for at least half an hour.

3 Remove the tuna from the marinade. Build the skewers, alternating the tuna with the tomatoes, artichoke hearts, and onion, placing a tuna cube between each vegetable piece. Grill over direct medium-high heat, turning frequently, 6 to 7 minutes or until the tuna is medium-rare and the vegetables are seared.

1½ pounds tuna steak, cut into 24 (1-ounce) cubes

½ cup olive oil

Juice of 1 lemon

1 teaspoon minced garlic

1 teaspoon sweet paprika

Coarse salt and freshly ground black pepper

3 small tomatoes, quartered

3 artichoke hearts, quartered

1 small red onion, cut into 12 wedges

Scallop and Ham Kabobs

Here's a different take on surf 'n' turf! Sweet sea scallops are the perfect foil for salty ham.

PREP TIME: 10 mins ★ GRILL TIME: 41 mins ★ SERVES 4

1 cup apricot jam
1 cup pineapple juice
Juice of 1 lemon
2 tablespoons peanut oil
1 tablespoon curry powder
Salt and pepper
24 large sea scallops
16 (1½-inch) cubes cooked ham

1 Combine the jam and half of the pineapple juice in a blender and process to a smooth puree. Add the remaining pineapple juice, the lemon juice, peanut oil, and curry powder and process to blend. Season with salt and pepper to taste. Add ham and scallops and toss to coat. Cover and refrigerate 30 minutes.

2 Preheat and oil the grill. Cover 8 bamboo skewers with water and soak at least half an hour.

3 Build the kabobs, alternating 3 scallops and 2 pieces of ham on each skewer. Grill over direct medium-high heat, turning frequently, about 4 minutes or until the scallops are cooked through and the ham is glazed.

Chef's Tip: All about Skewers

At one time, skewers were available in one shape (straight) and in one material (stainless steel). Now skewers are sold in different shapes (twig-shaped, circular, double-pronged) and materials (cast iron, bamboo, various other woods such as cedar and mesquite). You can even find them flavored with wine or herbs. Visit grilling- or cooking-supply stores to learn about all of the available options.

Brochettes of Shrimp and Papaya

Mango or pineapple make excellent substitutes for the papaya.

PREP TIME: 15 mins ★ GRILL TIME: 5 mins ★ SERVES 4

1 Whisk together the peanut oil, citrus juices, garlic, syrup, sake, ginger, and mint in a small bowl. Season with salt and pepper to taste. Place the shrimp and papaya in a glass baking dish and and pour the marinade over. Turn to coat, cover, and refrigerate 1 hour.

2 Preheat and oil the grill. Cover 8 bamboo skewers with water and soak at least half an hour.

3 For each skewer, alternate 3 shrimp and 2 pieces of papaya. Grill over direct medium-high heat, turning frequently, about 4 minutes or until the shrimp is cooked through and the papaya is glazed. Heat the marinade in a small saucepan over medium heat, and bring to a simmer. Remove from the heat and keep warm. Place 2 skewers on each serving plate. Drizzle with the warm marinade and garnish with lime wedges.

½ cup peanut oil

Juice of 2 limes

2 tablespoons freshly squeezed orange juice

2 cloves garlic, minced

1 tablespoon pure maple syrup

2 teaspoons sake

1 teaspoon grated fresh ginger

1 teaspoon chopped fresh mint

Salt and pepper

24 large shrimp, peeled and deveined

2 papayas, peeled, seeded, and cut into 1½-inch cubes

1 lime, cut into 8 wedges

Lemon-Chipotle Vegetable Kabobs

A filling vegetarian main course, these kabobs are also a colorful and tasty side dish for grilled meats and poultry. For even more Southwest flavor, use the Savory Spice Rub (page 23), lime juice in place of the lemon juice, and cilantro in place of the rosemary. You can also use different colors of bell peppers and golden tomatoes. Be creative!

PREP TIME: 15 mins ★ GRILL TIME: 10 mins ★ MAKES 8 kabobs

½ cup freshly squeezed lemon juice

½ cup olive oil

2 tablespoons fresh garlic, chopped

2 tablespoons fresh rosemary, chopped

Salt and pepper

¼ cup canned chipotle in adobo sauce, pureed

16 button mushroom caps

16 (1-inch) slices zucchini

1 red bell pepper, seeded, and cut into 1-inch squares

16 (1-inch) slices yellow squash

16 cherry tomatoes

½ cup Sweet Spice Rub (see page 23)

1 Cover eight 12-inch bamboo skewers with water and let soak at least half an hour.

2 Whisk together the lemon juice, oil, garlic, rosemary, and chipotle puree. Season with salt and pepper to taste.

3 Use two pieces of each vegetable on each skewer: a mushroom, then zucchini, pepper, yellow squash, then a cherry tomato; repeat. Place kabobs in a glass baking dish. Add the marinade, cover, and let stand 2 hours, turning occasionally so all sides are coated.

4 Preheat and oil the grill. Remove kabobs from marinade. Sprinkle kabobs with Sweet Spice Rub. Grill over medium indirect heat about 3 minutes per side or until vegetables are marked and crisp-tender.

Sides

Grilled Asparagus and Spring Onions

These grilled vegetables are the epitome of summery grilled flavor.
The vinaigrette is also delicious as a dressing on a green salad.

PREP TIME: 5 mins ★ GRILL TIME: 8 mins ★ SERVES 4 to 6

1 pound asparagus, trimmed, with the ends peeled clean

1 pound very small spring onions or large scallions, trimmed

1 cup extra-virgin olive oil

Salt and pepper

2½ tablespoons champagne vinegar

1½ tablespoons Dijon mustard

1 Preheat and oil the grill. Combine the asparagus and onions on a baking sheet. Add ½ cup oil and season with salt and pepper to taste, tossing to coat well.

2 Place the vegetables crosswise on the grid and grill over direct medium-high heat, turning frequently, for about 8 minutes or until crisp-tender and nicely caramelized.

3 Meanwhile combine the vinegar and mustard in a small bowl, whisking to combine. Slowly add the remaining ½ cup of oil, whisking constantly. Season with salt and pepper to taste.

4 Remove the vegetables from the grill and place on a serving platter. Drizzle with the dressing and serve.

Chef's Tip: Grilled Red Onions

Cut the top and bottom off of 2 large red onions and peel them. Cut the onions crosswise into ¾-inch-thick slices (you'll get 4 or 5 slices from each onion). Brush both sides of each slices with vegetable oil, then season both sides with salt and pepper to taste. Grill over indirect medium-high heat 5 to 7 minutes on each side or until onion is tender and has begun to caramelize.

Creamed Spinach

Even people who claim not to like spinach love this steakhouse classic. You can use 2 pounds of fresh spinach in place of the frozen spinach. Discard any wilted leaves and trim tough stems. Rinse well in several changes of cool water; do not dry. Proceed with the recipe as written.

PREP TIME: 10 mins ★ COOK TIME: 10 mins ★ SERVES 4 to 6

1 Place the spinach in a large saucepan with a lid. Cover and cook about 4 minutes or until the spinach has wilted. Remove from the heat and drain well, squeezing out all excess liquid.

2 Transfer the spinach to the bowl of a food processor fitted with a metal blade and pulse just until chopped.

3 Transfer the chopped spinach to a saucepan and stir in the butter. Add the cream and nutmeg, and cook over medium heat, stirring frequently, about 5 minutes or until the cream has thickened and the mixture is heated through. Season with salt and pepper to taste and serve hot.

> 2 (10-ounce) boxes frozen spinach, thawed and drained well
> 2 tablespoons unsalted butter
> ½ cup heavy (whipping) cream
> Pinch freshly ground nutmeg
> Salt and pepper

Wilted Mustard Greens

These greens have a flavor and a lively kick that matches well with the rich flavor of beef and lamb.

PREP TIME: 10 mins ★ COOK TIME: 15 mins ★ SERVES 4

1½ pounds mustard greens
1 tablespoon unsalted butter
1 shallot, minced
2 cloves garlic, minced
½ teaspoon coarse salt
½ teaspoon freshly ground
   black pepper

1 Prepare an ice bath in a large bowl.

2 Bring a large saucepan of water to a boil. With a sharp knife, remove the stems and coarse ribs of the mustard greens. Add the greens to the boiling water and use a wooden spoon to keep the leaves submerged. Cook about 5 minutes, or just until the leaves are wilted and tender.

3 Drain the greens and immediately transfer to the ice bath. Turn the leaves gently in the water to cool all of them. When cooled, strain in a colander, gently turning and pressing with the spoon to drain as much moisture as possible. Roughly chop the greens.

4 Melt the butter in a large sauté pan and add the shallot and garlic. Sauté over medium heat for 3 to 4 minutes, until softened. Add the chopped mustard greens, salt, and pepper. Cook for about 5 minutes longer, until warmed through.

Chef's Tip: Grilled Radicchio

Remove outer leaves from radicchio and trim woody ends. Quarter each head lengthwise. Brush radicchio with olive oil and season with salt and pepper to taste. Grill radicchio over indirect medium-high heat, covered, turning every 10 minutes, 25 to 30 minutes total, until outer leaves are browned and hearts are tender. Drizzle with balsamic vinegar and serve hot or at room temperature.

Grilled Parmesan Tomatoes

One tomato is usually enough for a serving, but these are so tasty we suggest you make a couple of extras. Brown the tops under a preheated broiler if you want a crunchier crust.

PREP TIME: 10 mins ★ GRILL TIME: 3 mins ★ SERVES 4

1 Preheat and oil the grill. Combine the bread crumbs, Parmesan, and basil in a small mixing bowl. Spoon equal portions of the mixture on the cut side of each tomato. Drizzle with the melted butter and season with salt and pepper to taste.

2 Grill the tomatoes, cut side up, over medium indirect heat for 3 to 4 minutes, or until the tops are bubbling. Remove from the grill and serve.

1/2 cup fresh bread crumbs

3 tablespoons freshly grated Parmesan cheese

1 tablespoon chopped fresh basil leaves

4 to 6 large ripe but firm tomatoes, cut in half

2 tablespoons unsalted butter, melted

Salt and pepper

Grilled Sweet and Sour Beets

Even people that claim not to like beets will not be able to resist the smoky sweetness of these grilled beets. For a shortcut version, use vacuum-packed cooked and peeled beets (look for them in the produce section). Beets that are all about the same size are best; they will cook at the same rate.

PREP TIME: 10 mins ★ GRILL TIME: 5 mins ★ SERVES 4 to 6

1 Combine the oil with the vinegars in a large bowl, whisking to blend. Whisk in the brown sugar and garlic until blended and the sugar has dissolved.

2 Add the beets; toss to coat. Season with salt and pepper to taste. Let stand 30 minutes, tossing occasionally. Preheat and oil the grill.

3 Grill the beets about 5 minutes, turning occasionally, or until nicely glazed. Serve hot or at room temperature.

½ cup olive oil

½ cup balsamic vinegar

1 tablespoon red wine vinegar

2 tablespoons light brown sugar

1 tablespoon minced garlic

2 pounds cooked beets, peeled and quartered

Salt and pepper

Chef's Tip: Grilled Fennel

Peel the outer layer from 2 medium fennel bulbs. Trim the tops, leaving about 3 inches of the green stalks. Cut each bulb in half vertically. Brush with olive oil, season with salt and pepper, and grill, cut side down about 4 minutes or until marked and slightly soft. Turn and grill the other side until marked and cooked through, about 2 minutes longer.

Grilled Red Chile Corn

Cooking the corn in the husks keeps the corn from drying out and the seasonings from burning.

PREP TIME: 10 mins ★ GRILL TIME: 20 mins ★ SERVES 4

4 ears fresh sweet corn, husks attached and silk removed

½ cup unsalted butter, at room temperature

1 tablespoon freshly squeeed lime juice

1 tablespoon pure red chile powder

½ tablespoon sweet paprika

1 teaspoon coarse salt

1 Place the corn in a large bowl of warm water and soak 1 hour. Preheat and oil the grill.

2 Stir together the butter, lime juice, chile powder, paprika, and salt in a small bowl until blended. Peel the corn husks back and spread a generous amount of the butter mixture over the kernels. Fold the husks back over the kernels. Grill over direct medium-high heat 20 to 25 minutes, turning occasionally. Serve with the husks still attached (for a handle).

Cowboy Cornbread

Grilling gives cornbread a satisfyingly toasty flavor reminiscent of chuck wagon cooking.

PREP TIME: 20 mins ★ GRILL TIME: 45 mins ★ SERVES 4

2 ears fresh sweet corn, husks attached and silk removed

1 tablespoon olive oil

2 cups cornmeal

1 cup all-purpose flour

½ tablespoon baking powder

½ tablespoon coarse salt

1 teaspoon baking soda

1 cup buttermilk

1 cup half-and-half

3 eggs

½ cup plus 1 tablespoon unsalted butter, melted and cooled

2 red jalapeño chiles, seeded and minced

2 green jalapeño chiles, seeded and minced

3 tablespoons chopped fresh cilantro

1 Preheat and oil the grill. Peel the corn husks back and brush the kernels with olive oil. Fold the husks back over the kernels. Grill over indirect medium heat 15 minutes, turning frequently, until lightly browned on all sides. Remove the corn from the grill and let cool. When cool enough to handle, cut the kernels from the cobs and set aside.

2 Combine the cornmeal, flour, baking powder, salt, and baking soda in a large bowl. Whisk together the buttermilk, half-and-half, and eggs in a medium bowl. Whisk in ½ cup melted butter. Pour the mixture over the dry ingredients. Stir in the corn kernels, jalapeños, and cilantro.

3 Set a large cast-iron skillet on the grill 2 minutes or until hot. Add the remaining 1 tablespoon butter to the skillet and swirl to coat the inside of the skillet. Pour in the batter and set the skillet over indirect heat. Cook, covered, 30 to 35 minutes or until golden brown and a toothpick inserted in the middle comes out clean. Serve cornbread warm in the skillet.

Polenta Sticks

This recipe transforms a northern Italian staple into an American barbecue classic. You can use crumbled blue cheese instead of the Parmesan, which would be a perfect match for the Filet Mignon with Compound Butter (page 47).

PREP TIME: **5 mins** ★ COOK TIME: **35 mins** ★ GRILL TIME: **6 mins** ★ SERVES **4**

1 Butter a 9-inch square baking pan. Combine the broth and milk in a large saucepan and bring to a boil over high heat. Stirring constantly with a wire whisk, gradually add the cornmeal in a steady stream. Whisk until the mixture thickens, 10 to 12 minutes.

2 Reduce the heat to low and simmer 20 minutes, stirring often. Stir in the Parmesan, butter, salt, and pepper. Transfer the polenta to the prepared pan, smoothing it into an even layer with a spatula. Cover and refrigerate 3 hours or overnight.

3 Preheat and oil the grill.

4 Turn the polenta out of the pan onto a work surface. Cut into sticks measuring about 3 inches long and 1 inch wide. Brush sticks with olive oil and place them crosswise on the grill. Cook over direct medium-high heat 3 or 4 minutes on each side or until golden brown and crisp. Serve warm.

> 3 cups chicken broth
> 2 cups milk
> 1 cup cornmeal
> 1/2 cup freshly grated Parmesan cheese
> 2 tablespoons unsalted butter
> 1 teaspoon coarse salt
> 1/2 teaspoon freshly ground black pepper
> 2 teaspoons olive oil

Spicy Homemade Applesauce

Once you've tasted this hot and sweet applesauce, you will always make your own. It doesn't take long, and the flavor and texture are so much more satisfying than the kind you buy in jars.

PREP TIME: **10 mins** ★ COOK TIME: **15 mins** ★ SERVES **4**

6 tart green apples (such as Granny Smith), peeled, cored, and chopped

½ cup chicken broth

2 tablespoons apple cider vinegar

1 tablespoon balsamic vinegar

½ teaspoon ground cumin

½ teaspoon ground coriander

1 head roasted garlic (see page 44)

3 tablespoons pure maple syrup

Salt and cayenne pepper

Combine the apples, chicken broth, vinegars, cumin, and coriander in a medium heavy saucepan. Add the roasted garlic flesh and cook over medium heat, stirring frequently, about 15 minutes or until the apples are mushy. Remove from the heat and stir in the syrup, salt, and cayenne to taste. Let cool to room temperature before serving.

Boston-Style Baked Beans

Historians believe that baked beans were first introduced to the Pilgrims by Native Americans. Whatever the origin, beans have long been a staple of New England cooking. We call for the beans to be soaked overnight, but you can do a quick soak (see below) if you're short on time.

PREP TIME: 20 mins ★ COOK TIME: 3 hours ★ SERVES 4

1 Preheat the oven to 300°F.

2 Drain and rinse the beans. Combine them with the water in a large saucepan over medium-high heat. Bring to a boil, then reduce the heat to medium and stir in the remaining ingredients. Bring to a simmer, then remove from heat. Transfer mixture to a casserole or large covered baking dish and bake 1 hour.

3 Stir the beans, adding a little more water if necessary. Cover and bake another hour. Stir, adding more water if necessary, and bake 1 hour longer or until the beans are tender. Season with salt to taste and serve.

2 cups dried navy beans, picked through and soaked overnight
6 cups cold water, plus more if necessary
4 ounces thick-cut (slab) bacon, diced
1 onion, diced
1/2 cup maple syrup (grade B), or dark molasses
1 cup chopped canned tomatoes
1 tablespoon dark brown sugar
1/2 tablespoon dry mustard powder
1/2 tablespoon Worcestershire sauce
1 teaspoon coarse salt, plus more to taste

Chef's Tip: Quick Soak for Dried Beans

Rinse the beans under cold water and discard any discolored ones and debris. Combine the beans with enough cold water to cover them by 2 inches in a large saucepan. Bring the beans to a boil over high heat, and boil 2 minutes. Remove from the heat, cover, and let the beans soak 1 hour. Drain and rinse beans before proceeding.

Peter Luger's German-Style Hash Brown Potatoes

These potatoes were created at Peter Luger, a Brooklyn steakhouse that has been in business since 1887. For the total Luger's experience (without making the trip to Brooklyn), serve them alongside the Double Porterhouse (see page 44) and Creamed Spinach (see page 147); both are on Luger's menu.

PREP TIME: 20 mins ★ COOK TIME: 45 mins ★ SERVES 4 to 6

1 Preheat the oven to 400°F. Fill a large bowl half-full with cold water. Peel the potatoes and slice them into ½-inch strips. Place the strips in the water as they are cut to keep them from turning brown. Drain the potato strips and pat them dry.

2 Line a baking sheet with paper towels. Add vegetable oil to a depth of ¾ inch into a large skillet and heat over medium heat until close to boiling. Working in 3 batches, fry the potatoes 10 to 12 minutes or until light golden brown. Remove the potatoes with a slotted spoon or strainer and spread on the paper towels to drain and cool. When the potatoes are cool enough to handle, cut them into ¼-inch dice.

3 Pour off all but 2 tablespoons of the oil from the skillet. Heat the oil over medium-high heat. Add the onions, paprika, and salt to taste. Sauté over medium-high heat 6 to 8 minutes, or until the onions start to soften and brown.

4 Melt the butter in a large ovenproof skillet. Add the potatoes and stir to mix. Cook, stirring, over medium-high heat until browned. Season with salt and pepper to taste. Add the onions and toss to mix. Transfer the skillet to the oven and roast 10 to 15 minutes or until crisp. Sprinkle with chopped parsley and serve.

5 large Idaho potatoes
Vegetable oil
1½ cups chopped onions
½ teaspoon sweet paprika
6 tablespoons unsalted butter
Salt and ground white pepper
Chopped fresh parsley, for garnish

Chef's Tip: Coal-Baked Potatoes

Prick each potato several times with a fork. Rub each potato with 1 tablespoon olive oil, then double wrap in aluminum foil. When the fire is still too hot to cook over but the flames have subsided, place the potatoes around the edges of the hot coals and roast 30 to 40 minutes or until soft.

Grilled Rosemary Potatoes

We bake these potatoes first so that they are almost cooked. Though this may seem like extra work, it produces fully cooked potatoes that have a crisp, grill-flavored exterior.

PREP TIME: **10 mins** ★ COOK TIME: **20 mins** ★ GRILL TIME: **10 mins** ★ SERVES **4**

---

4 large russet potatoes, scrubbed and cut into 1/2-inch-thick wedges

1/2 cup extra-virgin olive oil

1 tablespoon balsamic vinegar

1 tablespoon chopped fresh rosemary

Salt and pepper

---

1 Preheat the oven to 375°F. Preheat and oil the grill.

2 Arrange potatoes on a nonstick baking sheet. Sprinkle with olive oil, vinegar, rosemary, and salt and pepper to taste, tossing to coat well. Bake about 20 minutes or until almost cooked through.

3 Transfer the potato wedges to the grill. Grill over direct medium heat, turning frequently, about 10 minutes or until cooked through and nicely charred around the edges. Remove the potatoes from the grill, season with salt and pepper to taste, and serve hot.

Glazed Sweet Potatoes

The sprinkling of sea salt on the cooked glazed potatoes is a must.

PREP TIME: **10 mins** ★ COOK TIME: **15 mins** ★ GRILL TIME: **6 mins** ★ SERVES **4**

---

4 large sweet potatoes, scrubbed and cut into 1/2-inch-thick slices

1/2 cup olive oil

Coarse salt and ground black pepper

1/2 cup pure maple syrup

1/4 cup unsalted butter

1/2 teaspoon ground cinnamon

1/2 teaspoon ground cloves

Coarse sea salt

---

1 Preheat the oven to 375°F. Preheat and oil the grill.

2 Arrange sweet potatoes on a nonstick baking sheet. Add the oil and season with salt and pepper to taste, tossing to coat well. Bake for about 12 minutes or until almost cooked.

3 Meanwhile, heat the syrup, butter, cinnamon, and cloves in a small saucepan over low heat. Cook, stirring constantly, until smooth. Remove from the heat and keep warm.

4 Remove the potatoes from the oven and spoon the glaze mixture over the top, coating all the slices. Let cool slightly.

5 Grill the potato slices over medium-high direct heat for about 3 minutes on each side or until cooked through and nicely glazed. Remove from the grill, sprinkle with coarse sea salt to taste, and serve hot.

Arugula-Mango Salad with Herb-Lime Vinaigrette

It's important to wash arugula well as its leaves can sometimes be gritty. Arugula is sometimes sold as "rocket," so if you have trouble locating it in your market, look for it under that name.

PREP TIME: **15 mins** ★ SERVES **4**

1 Combine the lime juice, shallot, marjoram, garlic, salt, pepper, and brown sugar in a medium bowl. Gradually whisk in the olive oil until thoroughly incorporated.

2 Place the arugula in a salad bowl and add the onion and mango. Add half the vinaigrette and toss together to mix well. Serve right away with any remaining vinaigrette on the side.

---

2 tablespoons freshly squeezed lime juice

1 tablespoon minced shallot

1 tablespoon minced fresh marjoram

1 clove garlic, minced

1/2 teaspoon coarse salt

1/2 teaspoon freshly ground black pepper

Pinch brown sugar

1/2 cup olive oil

8 ounces arugula, stemmed

1/2 cup finely sliced red onion

1 mango, peeled, pitted, and finely diced

Quinoa Salad

Quinoa's nutty flavor goes well with grilled salmon. This salad can be prepared up to 3 or 4 hours ahead of time and served at room temperature or chilled.

PREP TIME: 15 mins ★ COOK TIME: 25 mins ★ SERVES 4

3 cups water

1/2 teaspoon coarse salt

1 tablespoon plus 2 teaspoons olive oil, divided

1 1/2 cups quinoa (about 10 ounces), rinsed and drained

1 tablespoon freshly squeezed lime juice

1/2 cup minced cucumber

1/2 cup each minced red, yellow, and green bell pepper

1 scallion, sliced

2 tablespoons minced fresh oregano

Freshly ground black pepper

1 Heat the water and salt in a medium saucepan until boiling. Meanwhile, heat 2 teaspoons of the oil in a separate medium saucepan over medium heat. Add the quinoa and stir for 1 minute until coated. Pour the boiling water over the quinoa. Return to a boil, partially cover the pan, and reduce the heat to low.

2 Simmer quinoa 15 minutes or until al dente. Drain any excess water, transfer the quinoa to a bowl, and let cool.

3 Whisk together the lime juice and 1 tablespoon of the olive oil in a medium bowl. Add the cucumber, bell peppers, scallion, oregano, and cooled quinoa. Season with pepper to taste and toss together. Serve hot or refrigerate up to 4 hours.

Creamy Slaw

Feel free to increase or decrease the herbs, garlic, or lemon juice to suit your tastes. If you have time, let this cole slaw stand at room temperature for 30 minutes to let the cabbage absorb some of the dressing.

PREP TIME: 5 mins ★ SERVES 4

1/2 cup sour cream

1/2 cup mayonnaise

2 tablespoons freshly squeezed lemon juice

2 tablespoons minced fresh flat-leaf parsley

1/2 teaspoon minced garlic

1 tablespoon grainy Dijon mustard

Salt and pepper

1 pound packaged cole slaw mix (with cabbage and carrots)

1 red onion, finely sliced

1 Whisk the sour cream and mayonnaise in a medium bowl intil blended. Whisk in the lemon juice, 1 tablespoon parsley, the garlic, and mustard. Season with salt and pepper to taste. Cover and refrigerate 1 hour.

2 Toss the cole slaw mix and onion in a large bowl until mixed. Add the chilled dressing and toss well to coat. Season with salt and pepper to taste. Let stand at room temperature 30 minutes before serving. Garnish with the remaining 1 tablespoon parsley just before serving.

Spiced Waldorf Salad

Here is our fresh take on a classic American favorite.
Add the walnuts just before serving so they stay crisp.

PREP TIME: 10 mins ★ SERVES 4 to 6

1 Whisk together the mayonnaise, crème fraîche, cider, oil, curry powder, and cayenne in a small bowl until smooth.

2 Combine the apples, celery root, and grapes in a medium mixing bowl, tossing to mix. Pour the mayonnaise mixture over the top and toss until coated.

3 If serving immediately, add the walnuts and toss to mix. If not serving immediately, cover and refrigerate up to 3 hours.

½ cup mayonnaise
½ cup crème fraîche or sour cream
1 tablespoon apple cider
1 teaspoon walnut or peanut oil
½ teaspoon curry powder
½ teaspoon cayenne pepper, or to taste
2 cups diced crisp apples
1 cup diced celery root
½ cup halved seedless red grapes
½ cup toasted walnut pieces

Warm Potato Salad

Stir in ½ cup chopped bacon bits to this salad for a little extra crunch and smoky flavor. This salad must be served warm, so if time is an issue, mix the dressing ingredients ahead and cook the potatoes just before serving.

PREP TIME: 10 mins ★ COOK TIME: 30 mins ★ SERVES 4

1½ pounds new potatoes, scrubbed
½ cup mayonnaise, or to taste
½ cup sour cream, or to taste
1 tablespoon Dijon mustard
3 tablespoons white vinegar
1 tablespoon chopped fresh flat-leaf parsley leaves
½ cup minced red onion
Salt and pepper

1 Place the potatoes in cold, salted water to cover in a medium saucepan. Place over high heat and bring to a boil. Cover, lower the heat, and simmer about 30 minutes or until just barely tender when pierced with the point of a small, sharp knife.

2 Meanwhile, stir together the mayonnaise, sour cream, and mustard in a small bowl. Whisk in the vinegar until smooth. Stir in the parsley.

3 Place the onion in a medium bowl.

4 Remove the potatoes from the heat and drain well. Carefully cut into quarters and add to the onion. Work quickly, as you want the potatoes to remain hot.

5 Pour the mayonnaise mixture over the potatoes and onion, tossing to coat well. Season with salt and pepper to taste and serve warm.

Chef's Tip: Potato 101

We used red-skinned potatoes for this recipe, but you could use any waxy potato here. Check out your local farmers' market for new and different potato varieties: Yukon Golds, fingerling, and blue potatoes would all add flavor and visual interest to this classic dish. (We do not advise using starchy potatoes, such as russets, however; they will not hold their shape in potato salad—save them for baking and mashing.)

Desserts

Pound Cake with Whipped Cream and Berries ★ 166

S'mores ★ 167

Spiced Mixed Fruit with Caramel Sauce ★ 168

Pineapple with Rum-Raisin Sauce ★ 169

Maple Peaches with Cream ★ 170

Figs with Mascarpone Cheese and Toasted Walnuts ★ 170

Pound Cake with Whipped Cream and Berries

If you have a prepared pound cake on hand, this is a terrific last-minute dessert.
Homemade pound cake works too, of course.

PREP TIME: 10 mins ★ GRILL TIME: 3 mins ★ SERVES 4

4 (1/2-inch-thick) slices
  pound cake
2 cups sliced strawberries or a
  mix of sliced strawberries and
  other seasonal berries
1/2 cup heavy cream, lightly
  whipped
1 tablespoon chopped fresh
  mint leaves

1 Preheat the grill.

2 Grill the pound cake slices over direct medium heat about 3 minutes, or until warm and nicely marked by the grill, turning frequently to keep the cake from charring.

3 Arrange the slices of pound cake on a platter. Spoon the berries over the top, then spoon the whipped cream over all. Sprinkle the mint over the top and serve.

Chef's Tip: Sour Cream Pound Cake

Preheat oven to 350°F. Grease and flour an 8 1/2 x 4 1/2-inch loaf pan. Whisk together 1 1/2 cups all-purpose flour, 1/8 teaspoon baking soda, and 1/8 teaspoon salt in a medium bowl and set aside. Using a mixer on high speed, cream 1/2 cup softened unsalted butter and 1 1/2 cups sugar until light and fluffy. With the mixer on low, beat in a heaping 1/2 cup sour cream, 3 eggs, and 1/2 teaspoon vanilla extract, mix until blended. Stir in the dry ingredients until blended and smooth. Pour batter into the prepared pan. Bake 1 hour 15 minutes or until a toothpick inserted into the center of the cake comes out clean. Let cool in the pan 1 hour, then turn out onto a wire rack to cool completely before slicing.

S'mores

Use handmade or flavored marshmallows for an update on this traditional campfire treat.
We've given directions for one s'more, but you can make as many as you like!

GRILL TIME: 2 min ★ SERVES 1

1 Preheat the grill.

2 Place a graham cracker on a work surface. Cover with a square of chocolate and top with almonds. Skewer a marshmallow and hold about 6 inches above the hot grill. Grill, turning constantly, about 1 minute or until hot, puffed, and lightly browned. Transfer to a chocolate-topped graham cracker. Cover with a plain graham cracker and transfer the whole "sandwich" to the hot grill. Grill 30 seconds, turn, and grill another 30 seconds or until the chocolate just begins to ooze out.

3 Remove from the grill and eat immediately. Keep making s'mores until you can't eat any more!

For each S'more:
2 graham crackers
One 2-inch square dark chocolate
1/2 teaspoon chopped toasted almonds
1 large marshmallow

Spiced Mixed Fruit with Caramel Sauce

This is a great fall or winter dessert when fresh fruit is not at its best.
You can make your own caramel, if you like; you'll need about 2 cups for this recipe.

PREP TIME: 15 mins ★ COOK TIME: 15 mins ★ GRILL TIME: 6 mins ★ SERVES 4

For the Spiced Mixed Fruit:

1 pound mixed dried fruit halves, such as peaches, pears, apricots

½ cup light brown sugar

1 cup dry white wine

5 whole cloves

2 whole star anise

1 cinnamon stick

½ cup unsalted butter, melted

½ cup chopped toasted pecans

For the Caramel Sauce:

2 cups bottled caramel sauce (or homemade, below)

1 tablespoon freshly squeezed lemon juice, strained

1 tablespoon vanilla extract

1 **For the Mixed Fruit,** preheat and oil the grill. Place the dried fruit in a heatproof bowl and cover with at least 2 cups of boiling water. Set aside 30 minutes to plump. Drain well, reserving 1 cup of the soaking liquid.

2 Combine the fruit, reserved soaking liquid, and brown sugar in a large nonreactive saucepan over medium heat. Add the wine, cloves, star anise, and cinnamon stick. Bring to a simmer and let simmer about 10 minutes or until the fruit is soft.

3 Remove the pan from the heat and strain through a fine mesh sieve, discarding the whole spices.

4 Lightly brush the fruit with melted butter. Grill in a basket over direct medium-high heat about 6 minutes, turning occasionally, or until nicely glazed.

5 **Meanwhile, for the Caramel Sauce,** heat the caramel sauce over low heat. Stir in lemon juice and vanilla. Keep warm until ready to serve.

6 Remove the fruit from the grill and divide evenly among 4 soup bowls. Drizzle with the caramel sauce, sprinkle with the chopped pecans, and serve warm.

Chef's Tip: Homemade Caramel Sauce

Combine 1 cup packed light brown sugar and ³/₄ cup granulated sugar with 1 cup cold water in a heavy saucepan over medium heat. Bring to a boil. Boil without stirring, brushing down the sides of the pan with a wet pastry brush to dissolve any sugar crystals that form, 12 minutes or until the syrup is a deep caramel color. Remove the pan from the heat and whisk in ¼ cup corn syrup, 1 tablespoon lemon juice, and 1 tablespoon vanilla extract, taking care that the mixture does not boil over. Bring to a simmer and carefully whisk in 1 ³/₄ cups heavy cream. Return the pan to the heat and bring to a boil. Reduce the heat and simmer about 10 minutes or until thick. Remove from the heat and serve warm.

Pineapple with Rum-Raisin Sauce

Fresh pineapple is best for this recipe, but you can also use well-drained, unsweetened canned pineapple slices.

PREP TIME: **10 mins** ★ COOK TIME: **6 mins** ★ GRILL TIME: **6 mins** ★ SERVES **4**

1 Preheat the grill. Place the raisins in a heatproof bowl and add boiling water to cover. Set aside 30 minutes to plump. Drain well.

2 Heat the butter in a small saucepan over medium heat. Add the brown sugar, rum, lemon juice, and five-spice powder. Cook, stirring constantly, about 5 minutes or until the sauce has thickened. Stir in the raisins and cook 1 minute longer.

3 Grill the pineapple over direct medium heat about 3 minutes on each side, or until very hot and nicely marked. Remove from the grill and cut into bite-sized pieces.

4 Divide the pineapple evenly among 4 dessert dishes. Top with sauce, sprinkle with nuts, and serve.

½ cup golden raisins
½ cup unsalted butter
½ cup light brown sugar
½ cup rum
2 teaspoons freshly squeezed lemon juice
½ teaspoon Chinese five-spice powder
1 pineapple, about 2 pounds, peeled, cored, and cut into ½-inch-thick slices
½ cup chopped toasted macadamia nuts

Maple Peaches with Cream

Peaches that are a little underripe work best in this recipe; the heat brings out their natural sugars.

PREP TIME: 10 mins ★ GRILL TIME: 5 mins ★ SERVES 4

½ cup sour cream

2 tablespoons light brown sugar

½ cup unsalted butter, melted

2 tablespoons pure maple syrup

Pinch ground nutmeg

4 large freestone peaches, cut in half lengthwise and pitted

1 Preheat the grill. Stir together the sour cream and brown sugar in a small bowl.

2 Combine the butter, syrup, and nutmeg in a small bowl. Lightly brush each peach half with the mixture. Grill the peaches over direct medium heat about 4 minutes, or until heated through and nicely glazed. Turn and grill the bottoms just until marked, about 1 minute.

3 Remove the peaches from the grill and place, cut side up, on a serving platter. Spoon some of the sugared sour cream on top of each half and serve.

Figs with Mascarpone and Toasted Walnuts

You can replace the figs with peaches, apricots, or any fruit you have available. Firmer, less ripe figs will take a little longer to grill. Don't forget the nutcracker!

PREP TIME: 5 mins ★ GRILL TIME: 25 mins ★ SERVES 4

16 walnuts in their shells

16 ripe figs

1 cup mascarpone cheese

2 tablespoons aged balsamic vinegar

1 Preheat the grill. Grill the walnuts over direct medium heat, turning occasionally, about 25 minutes.

2 About 10 minutes before the nuts are done, place the figs on the grill. Grill, turning carefully so they don't split, about 10 minutes or until hot and about to pop. Remove figs and walnuts from the grill.

3 Place ¼ cup mascarpone in the center of each of 4 dessert plates. Arrange 4 figs around the cheese on each plate. Drizzle the cheese with vinegar. Serve with the walnuts on the side.

Chef's Tip

Mascarpone cheese is a rich double-cream Italian cheese with a slightly tangy flavor. If you can't find it, substitute 1 cup whipped cream cheese sweetened with a little sugar.

Maple Peaches with Cream

Index